The Masonic Initiation

Titles in the
Agapa Masonic Classics series

The Meaning of Masonry
The Masonic Initiation
Walter Leslie Wilmshurst

The Symbolism of Freemasonry
Masonic Jurisprudence
Albert G. Mackey

The Philosophy of Freemasonry
Roscoe Pound

The Pythagorean Triangle:
Sacred Geometry in the Masonic Tradition
George Oliver

Symbolism of the Three Degrees of Freemasonry
Oliver Day Street

W. L. Wilmshurst

The Masonic Initiation

Revised and Expanded

Plumbstone | *San Francisco*

Agapa Masonic Classics presents modern editions
of important works relating to the history, philosophy
and interpretation of Freemasonry.

Originally published in 1924 by William Rider & Son, London.
Revised and expanded edition by Agapa Masonic Classics.

Wilmshurst, Walter Leslie, 1867-1939.
    The masonic initiation, Rev. ed. / W. L. Wilmshurst.
        p.   cm.
    ISBN 978-1-60302-003-9 (hardcover)
    ISBN 978-1-60302-002-2 (paperback)
    I. Title. II. Series: Agapa masonic classics.

http://www.plumbstone.com

To all Builders in the Spirit

Contents

Foreword

THERE are many books available which attempt to explain Masonic history, symbols, philosophy and ethics. In fact, there is more being written on Freemasonry today by both scholars and academicians than has been written in the past one hundred years. Perhaps this is a testament to a new and rapidly expanding interest and curiosity about the world's oldest fraternal society. But to a large extent, this new inquiry is inspired by a greater appreciation today for secret societies and a deeper understanding that the meanings behind life's essential questions must come from within the individual.

Still, there are relatively few works which focus on the spiritual dimensions of the ancient Craft—the mystic tradition as it really exists beneath the veil of Masonry's beautiful ritual language and ceremonial forms. For those who are motivated to consider the quest themes of Freemasonry—the path to living a full and beneficial life, the journey for truth—they would do well to start their adventure with Walter Wilmshurst's classic texts, *The Meaning of Masonry* and *The Masonic Initiation*.

Wilmshurst was one of the world's greatest Masons, deepest mystics, and renowned English gentlemen. When these books were originally written in the 1920s, they were warmly received by Masons everywhere. Now, this newly revised edition by Shawn Eyer, editor of the Agapa Masonic Classics series, offers a much easier to read typeface with footnotes clarifying the meaning of archaic words, explaining English ritual nuances not commonly found in American workings, and citing many literary and Biblical references not mentioned in the original text.

The result is an easy-to-read and gratifying set of important works which affirm Wilmshurst's interpretation: that the progressive lessons of Craft Masonry are nothing less than the spiritual journey of the psyche toward full realization.

Here the contemporary Mason is given a new look at two timeless classics which have induced many generations of Masons to feel that, when they are in the sacred space of lodge, they are in the presence of a mystery that goes to the root of their own being.

Robert G. Davis 33° G C

GUTHRIE, OKLAHOMA

Publisher's Foreword to the New Edition

INITIATION is the core of the Masonic experience, and few have ever written about the sublime nuances and shocking wonder of its processes like Walter Leslie Wilmshurst. He perceived the Craft as more than an elaborate display of moral values and common-sense lessons: by carefully listening to its ceremonies and opening his eyes to their powerful symbolism, he found uncommon wisdom and profound mystery.

While most interpreters of Freemasonry approach the topic with their philosophical biases too strongly applied, Wilmshurst's work generally transcends this regrettably common limitation. While making no apology for his personal spiritual commitments, Wilmshurst shares how he relates them intimately with his experience of the Craft in a manner that is straightforward, with a depth unmatched and sincerity unmistakable. He has kept the spirit of Freemasonry steadfastly in focus, the voice of the ritual itself resonating and penetrating. The result is this true classic among Masonic books.

In these pages we encounter an experienced guide like few others, who travels the lesser-known and least-explored territories of the Craft with ease. But the reader must remember that neither Wilmshurst nor any other writer can lead us directly to the essence of initiation: he can only provide hints, even if they are very powerful and vivid. The initiatic experience is not territory one may sprint across. "He who runs would not care to give careful attention," wrote another wise Mason, "and he who stops and thinks would better make the personal effort himself, and thus gain all the good in order to pass it on to someone else by throwing out the suggestion."* Ultimately, the personal and transformative quest of initiation can only

---

*   Thomas Milton Stewart, *Symbolic Teaching, or Masonry and Its Message* (Cincinnati: Steward & Kidd Company, 1915), p. 100.

be made within one's self, and Wilmshurst's valuable efforts to pass on his deepest insights will serve the reader handily as he travels.

Of particular note in these empowering and enlightening pages is Wilmshurst's description of his notion of the "ideal lodge"—one in which ritual is always performed in a contemplative mood, with the attention of the brethren firmly fixed on the serious and sacred goal of initiation. In his day, this understanding of Masonry led to the foundation of the openly contemplative Lodge of Living Stones in the English Midlands, a development that presaged the growing popularity in our own times of lodges with a traditional, philosophical emphasis. This resurgence of widespread interest in and appreciation for the esoteric aspects of Masonic philosophy is timely, and can only benefit a modern world that too often replaces the sacred with the profane, its values misplaced among the shifting sands of popular tides. The authenticity and worth of the Masonic tradition beckons members and nonmembers alike, and they are in luck if Wilmshurst is among their allies.

Another section of this book which should escape no reader's attention is the "Apocalypsis" in the third chapter. Here, Wilmshurst describes a visionary ascent to a place, or rather a state of mind, that Freemasons have traditionally termed the celestial lodge or the supreme grand lodge. Unparalleled in Masonic literature, this "dream sequence" tells a deeply personal tale of personal growth to which many philosophically-minded Masons of today will enthusiastically relate. Using a literary device strikingly similar to the Jewish merkavah mysticism of two millennia ago, Brother Wilmshurst attends the heavenly temple in his mind's eye, and walks among its celestial brethren. Yet even through such rarefied territory, Wilmshurst's writing is a paragon of restraint, and leaves us deeply moved and spiritually refreshed.

This is surely the key to Wilmshurst's lasting appeal. As Antony Baker expressed in his 2006 address before Quatuor

Coronati, the world's premier lodge of Masonic research, Wilmshurst has "left behind a series of books and papers which are a constant source of instruction and assistance to those who are seeking for that which was lost and which they hope some day to find."*

The perpetual popularity of Wilmshurst's first book, The Meaning of Masonry, makes it especially regrettable that this arguably superior sequel has not been read by most of today's Freemasons. Agapa Masonic Classics is delighted to offer this new edition through Plumbstone Books. The original text has been lightly modernized for the comfort of modern readers, and new references and footnotes have been added so that we may trace the author's many sources. Also, because Wilmshurst originally wrote for a British audience, aspects of the Masonic ritual that are found in England but not in America have been elucidated for the benefit of Masons in the United States and other jurisdictions.

---

* Antony R. Baker, "W. L. Wilmshurst: His World of Fallen but Living Stones," Ars Quatuor Coronatorum, vol. 119 (2006), p. 82. This article is highly recommended as the most thorough available examination of Wilmshurst's life and work. The author offers a vivid biographical sketch and presents a detailed analysis of the social, intellectual and philosophical ideas which influenced Wilmshurst's development. This is supplemented by a complete bibliography of Wilmshurst's writings, many of which are quite rare.

WISDOM alone is the right coin with which to deal, and with it everything of real worth is bought and sold. And for it, Temperance and Justice, Fortitude and Prudence, are a kind of preliminary purification.

And those who instituted the mysteries for us appear to have been by no means contemptible persons, and to have intimated in a veiled manner that whoever descends into Hades uninitiated, and without being a partaker in the mysteries, shall lie in the mire; but that whoever arrived there purified and initiated, shall dwell with the Gods. Yet, as said those who preside over the mysteries:

> "Many are the candidates seeking initiation,
> But few are the perfected initiates."

But these few are, in my judgment, true wisdom-lovers; and that I may be of their number I shall leave nothing unattempted, but shall exert myself in all possible ways.

—Socrates

Phaedo 69A – D

Introduction
Masonry and Religion

THIS BOOK is meant to be a sequel to, and an amplification of, my previous volume, *The Meaning of Masonry*—a collection of papers issued diffidently and tentatively on the chance that they might interest some few members of the Craft in the deeper and philosophical aspect of Freemasonry. It at once met, however, with a surprisingly warm welcome from all parts of the world, and already has had to be thrice reprinted. Any personal pleasure at its reception is eclipsed by a greater gratification and thankfulness at the now demonstrated fact that the present large and rapid increase in the number of the fraternity is being accompanied by a correspondingly wide desire to realize the significance and purpose of the Masonic system to a much fuller degree than till now has been the case. The Masonic Craft seems to be gradually regenerating itself, and, as I previously indicated, such a regeneration must necessarily make not only for the moral benefit and enlightenment of individuals and lodges, but ultimately must react favorably upon the framework in which they exist—the whole body of society.

In these circumstances it becomes possible to speak more fully, perhaps also more feelingly, upon a subject which, as a large volume of public and private testimony has revealed to me, is engaging the earnest interest of large numbers of brethren of the Craft. So I offer them these further papers, presenting the same subject matter as before, but in different form and expounding more fully matters previously treated but superficially and cursorily.

By "the Masonic initiation" I mean, of course, not merely the act and rite of reception into the Order, but speculative Freemasonry—within the limits of the Craft and Arch degrees—regarded as a system, a specialized method of intellectual guidance and spiritual instruction; a method which to its willing and attentive devotees offers at once an interpretation of life, a rule of living, and a means of grace, introduction, and even intromission, to life and light of a supra-natural order. Masonry being essentially and expressly a quest after supranatural Light, the present papers are schematically arranged in correspondence with the stages of that quest; they deal first with the transition from darkness to light; next with the pathway itself and the light to be found thereon; and, lastly, with light in its fullness of attainment as the result of faithfully pursuing that path to the end. In a final paper I have resurveyed the Order's past and indicated its present tendencies and future possibilities.

In their zeal to appreciate and make the best of their connection with the Order, some members, one finds, experience difficulty in defining and "placing" Freemasonry. Is it religion, philosophy, a system of morals, or what? In view of the deepening interest in the subject, it may be well at the outset to clear up this point. Masonry is not a religion, though it contains marked religious elements and many religious references. A brother may legitimately say, if he wishes—and many do say—"Masonry is my religion," but he is not justified in classifying and holding it out to other people as a religion. Reference to the Constitutions makes it quite clear that the system is one meant to exist outside and independently of religion; that all the Order requires of its members is a belief in Deity and personal conformation to the moral law, every brother being free to follow whatsoever form of religion and mode of worship he pleases.

Neither is Masonry a philosophy; albeit behind it lies a large philosophical background not appearing in its surface-rituals and doctrine, but left for discovery to the research and effort of the brethren. That philosophical background is a gnosis or wisdom-teaching as old as the world, one which has been shared alike by the Vedists of the East, the Egyptian, Chaldean and Orphic initiation systems, the Pythagorean and Platonist schools, and all the mystery temples of both the past and the present, Christian or otherwise. The present renaissance in the Masonic Order is calculated to cause a marked, if gradual, revival of interest in that philosophy, with the probable eventual result that there will come about a general restoration of the mysteries, inhibited during the last sixteen centuries. But of this more will be said in the final section of this book.

The official description of Masonry is that it is a "system of morality."* This is true, but in two senses, one only of which is usually thought of. The term is usually interpreted as meaning a "system of morals." But men need not enter a secret order to learn morals and study ethics; nor is an elaborate ceremonial organization needed to teach them. Elementary morals can be, and are, learned in the outside world; and must be learned there if one is to be merely a decent member of society. The possession of "strict morals," as every Mason knows, is a preliminary qualification for entering the Order; a man does not enter it to acquire them after he has entered. It is true he finds the Order insistent on obedience to the moral law and emphasizing closer cultivation of certain ethical virtues, as is essential to those who propose to enter upon a course of spiritual science; and this is the primary, more obvious sense in which the term "system of morality" is used.

But the word "morality," in its original, and also in its Masonic, connotation, has a further meaning; one carrying the same sense as it does when we speak of a "morality-play."

* Wilmshurst alludes to the classical definition of Freemasonry. In 1772 William Preston wrote, "The whole is one regular system of morality, conceived in a strain of interesting allegory, which unfolds its beauties to the candid and industrious inquirer." (See Preston's *Illustrations of Masonry*, 1772 edition, p. 60)—Ed.

A "morality" is a literary or dramatic way of expressing spiritual truth, putting it forward allegorically and in accordance with certain well-settled principles and methods (mores); it is the equivalent of a usage or "use," as ecclesiastics speak of "the Sarum use" or liturgy. In the same sense Plutarch's *Moralia* is largely a series of disquisitions upon the mores of the ancient religious mystery schools.

A "system of morality," therefore, means secondarily "a systematized and dramatized method of moral discipline and philosophical instruction, based on ancient usage and long established practice." The method in question is that of initiation; the usage and practice is that of allegory and symbol, which it is the Freemason's duty, if he wishes to understand his system, to labor to interpret and put into personal application. If he fails to do so, he still remains—and the system deliberately intends that he should—in the dark about the Order's real meaning and secrets, although formally a member of it. The Order, the morality-system, merely guarantees its own possession of Truth; it does not undertake to impart it save to those who labor for it. For Truth and its real *arcana* can never be communicated directly or otherwise, except through allegory and symbol, myth and sacrament. The onus of translating these must ever rest with the recipient as part of his lifework; until he *makes* the truth his own he can never *know* it to be truth; he must do the will before he can know the doctrine. "I know not how it is" (said St. Bernard of Clairvaux of allegory and symbol) "but the more that spiritual realities are clothed with obscuring veils, the more they delight and attract; and nothing so much heightens longing for them as such tender refusal."

Masonry, then—as a "system of morality" as thus defined—is neither a religion nor a philosophy, but at once a science and an art, a theory and a practice; and this was ever the way in which the schools of the ancient wisdom and mysteries proceeded. They first exhibited to the intending disciple a picture of life's process: they taught him the story of

the soul's genesis and descent into this world; they showed
him its present imperfect, restricted state and its unfortunate
position; they indicated that there was a scientific method
by which it might be perfected and regain its original condition. This was the science-half of their systems, the program
or theory placed in advance before disciples, that they might
have a thorough intellectual grasp of the purpose of the mysteries and what admission to them involved. Then followed
the other half: the practical work to be done by the disciple
upon himself, in purifying himself; controlling his sense-nature; correcting natural undisciplined tendencies; mastering
his thought, his mental processes and will, by a rigorous rule
of life and art of living. When he showed proficiency in both
the theory and the practice, and could withstand certain tests,
then—but not before—he was allowed the privilege of initiation: a secret process, conferred by already initiated Masters
or experts, the details of which were never disclosed outside
the process itself.

Such, in a few words, was the age-old science of the mysteries, whether in Egypt, Greece or elsewhere, and it is that
science which, in very compressed, diluted form, is perpetuated and reproduced in modern Masonry.* To emphasizing
and demonstrating this fact, both the present and my former
volume are devoted; their purpose being coupled with a hope
that, when the true intention of the Order is perceived, the
Craft may begin to fulfill its original design and become an
instrument of real initiating efficiency instead of, as hitherto,
a merely social and charitable institution. Indeed the place
and office of Masonry cannot be adequately appreciated without acquaintance with the mysteries of antiquity, for as a poet
wrote who knew the latter perfectly:

* For a valuable outline of the work of the mysteries, reference may be
  made to the recent (1918) reprint of *A Suggestive Inquiry into the Hermetic
  Mystery* by M. A. Atwood, with an extensive introduction to the subject
  from my own pen; published by Tait, Belfast, and Watkins, London.
  [This was originally published anonymously in 1850.—Ed.]

Save by the Old Road none attain the new,
And from the Ancient Hills alone we catch the view![*]

Masonry having the above purpose, while not a religion, is consistent with and adaptable to any and every religion. But it is capable of going further. For an Order of initiation (like the monastic Orders within the older churches) is intended to provide a higher standard of instruction, a larger communication of truth and wisdom, than the elementary ones offered by public popular religion; and at the same time it requires more rigorous personal discipline and imposes much more exacting claims upon the mind and will of its adherents. The popular religious teaching of any people, Christian or not, is as it were for the masses as yet incapable of stronger food and unadapted to rigorous discipline; it is accommodated to the simple understanding of the man in the street, jog-trotting along the road of life. initiation is meant for the expert, the determined spiritual athlete, ready to face the deeper mysteries of being, and resolute to attain, as soon as may be, the heights to which he knows his own spirit, when awakened, can take him.

Is not the present declension of interest in popular religion and public worship due—far from entirely, yet largely—not to irreligiosity, but to the fact that conventional religious presentation does not satisfy the rational and spiritual needs of a public forced and disciplined by the exigencies of modern existence to insist upon a clear understanding and a firm intellectual foothold in respect of any form of venture it is called upon to undertake? Is not the turn-over of so many essentially religiously-minded and earnestly questing people from the churches to variants of religious expression, including Masonry, due largely to that reason and to the fact that the churches, while inculcating faith, offering hope, pro-

* One of the "Fragments" in *The Poems of Coventry Patmore*, edited by Frederick Page (New York: Oxford University Press, 1949), p. 479.—Ed.

claiming love, fail entirely in providing what the mysteries of the past always did—such a clear philosophical explanation of life and the universe as provided—not proof, which in regard to ultimate verities it is impossible to offer—but an intellectual motive for turning from things of sense to things of spirit?

Nothing is further from my wish or intention in these pages than to extol Masonry at the expense of any existing religion or church, or to suggest competition between institutions which are not and can never be competitors, but complementaries. I am merely asserting the simple obvious facts that popular favor has turned, and will more and more turn, to that market which best supplies its needs, and that for many nowadays the churches fail to supply those needs, or form at best an inferior or inadequate source of supply. The growing human intelligence has outgrown—not religious truth—but presentations of it that sufficed in less exacting social conditions than obtain today, and it is calling for more sustaining nutriment.

It may be useful to recall how the position was viewed not long ago by an advanced mind racially detached from the religion and ways of the Western world. A Hindu religious master, an initiate, who attended the World's Congress of Religions at Chicago† as the representative of the Vedantists, made an observational tour of America and Europe with a view to sympathetically understanding and appraising their religious organizations and methods. His conclusions may be summarized thus: "The Western ideal is to be doing (to be active); the Eastern, to be suffering (to be passive). The perfect life would be a wonderful harmony of the two. Western religious organizations (churches and sects) involve grave disadvantages; for they are always breeding new evils, which are not known to the East with its absence of organization. The perfect condition would come from a true blending of these opposite meth-

† This was the first event of its kind, held in 1893.—Ed.

ods. For the Western soul, it is well for a man to be born in a church, but terrible for him to die in one; for in religion there must be growth. A young man is to be censured who fails to attend and learn from the church of his nation; the elderly man is equally to be censured if he does attend—he ought to have outgrown what that church offers and to have attained a higher order of religious life and understanding."

The same conclusion was expressed by an eminent and ardent religionist of our own country: "The work of the Church in the world is *not to teach the mysteries of life*, so much as to persuade the soul to that arduous degree of purity at which Deity Himself becomes her teacher. The work of the Church ends when the knowledge of God begins."* In other words, initiation science (in a real and not merely a ceremonial sense) is needed and commences to be applicable only when elementary spiritual tuition has been assimilated and richer nourishment is called for. The same writer, though a zealous member of the Roman church, affirms frankly and truly that in any age of the world, the real initiate of the mysteries, whatever his race or national religion, must necessarily always stand higher in spiritual wisdom and stature than the non-initiate of the Christian or any other faith.

Such testimonies as these point to—what many others will feel to be a necessity—the need of some complementary, supplementary aid to popular religion; some higher grade school, in the greater seclusion and privacy of which can be both studied and practiced lessons in the secrets and mysteries of our being which cannot be exhibited *coram populo*. Such an aid is provided by a secret order, an initiation system, and is at hand in Freemasonry. It remains to be seen whether the Masonic Craft, in both its own and the larger ulterior interest of society, will avail itself of the opportunity in its hands. There

---

*   Coventry Patmore, *The Rod, the Root, and the Flower* (London: Bell, 1895).

being a tendency in that direction in the Craft today, the pages of this and of my former book are offered to encouraging that tendency to a fruition that could not make otherwise than for the general good.

But let those of us who are desirous to further that tendency, and to see provided an advanced system of spiritual instruction, never entertain a notion of *competing* with any other community, or permit ourselves a single thought of disparagement or contempt towards either those who learn or those who teach in other places. Life involves growth. The hyacynth-bulb in the pot before me will not remain a bulb, whose life and stature are to be restricted to the level of the pot it has been placed in. It will shoot up a foot higher and there burst in flower and fragrance, albeit that its roots remain in the soil. Similarly each human life is as a bulb providentially planted in some pot, in some religion, some church. If it truly fulfills the law and central instincts of its nature it will outgrow that pot, rise high above the pot's surface-level, and ultimately blossom in a consciousness transcending anything it knew while in the bulb stage. That consciousness will be one not of the beginner, the student, the neophyte in the mysteries; it will be that of the full initiate.

But that perfected life will still be rooted in the soil, and, far from despising it, will be for ever grateful for the pot in which its growth became possible. Masonry will, therefore, never disparage simpler or less advanced forms of intellectual or spiritual instruction. The Mason, above all men and in a much fuller, deeper sense, will respond to the old ordinance "honor thy father and mother." In whatever form, under whichsoever of the many names the God-idea presents itself to himself or his fellow-men, he will honor the Universal Father; and in whatsoever soil of mother earth, or whichsoever section of mother church, he or they have received their infant nurture, he will honor that mother, even as he is bound also to honor his own "mother lodge"; seeing in each of these the temporal reflection of still another Mother, the supernal parent described as "the Mother of us all."

Upon one other point I must add a word. A writer wishing to help on the understanding of Masonry, as fully as may be, in the interests of brethren who, as events have shown, are waiting in numbers to receive and ready to turn to account such help as may be given, is put to real anxiety to find a way of so writing that he simultaneously discharges the combined duty of extending that help and of observing his own obligations as to silence.

In my former volume I explained that, in respect of necessary safeguards, all due secrecy should be observed; and the assurance is now repeated in respect of the present one. No non-Mason need look to find in these pages any of the distinctive secrets of the Craft; no Mason, I believe, will trace in them any disloyal word or motive, or recognize in them anything but earnest anxiousness to promote the Craft's interests to the uttermost. Moreover the things I permit myself to say are, I conceive, exempt from silence as regards the Craft, for they are things which justly and lawfully belong to it and properly concern it; and since its members, near and far, in full measure and in many ways have proved themselves worthy of such confidence as I can show them, I feel myself justified in addressing them more intimately than before. As regards those outside the Craft, into whose hands a published book cannot be prevented from falling, what I have written consists of things already spoken about at large in other forms of expression in these days of keen search for guidance upon the dark path of human life; and let me here say that as warm, and almost as many, appreciations of my former volume have reached me from non-Masons as from within the Craft, and that it has attracted to the Order much sympathy and goodwill that did not previously exist.

Doubtless there are eyes of such strictness that they regard any public mention of the Masonic subject as an impropriety. Even these I would not willingly offend; yet to allow a possible technicality to prevent the giving, to those seeking it, the only gift I can make to the Craft in return for what it has given to myself, seems to me less meritorious Masonic conduct than would be the negative virtue of keeping rigid silence when so much can usefully be said.

So I take comfort from that ancient word of wisdom which proclaims that "he that observes the wind shall not sow, and he that observes the clouds will not reap!" (Ecclesiastes 11:4) And though, while writing these pages, a morning desire to sow my seed has often been followed by an evening prompting to withhold my hand, yet the former has prevailed with me. And if of that seed, some falls upon Masonic and some chances upon other ground, who shall know whether shall prosper this or that? But I pray that both shall be alike good. For, continues the same old sage, "truly Light is sweet, and a precious thing it is for the eyes to behold the Sun" (Ecclesiastes 11:7); and today there are drawn blinds everywhere waiting to be lifted, to let in a sunlight that belongs to no close community, but to all men alike.

So having, I hope, brought myself to order in this respect, and marking with thankful eyes the sunrise of a new order of intelligence breaking over the Brotherhood, let me now proceed, in the one Name that is thought of under many names, to declare the lodge open, for the purpose of considering Craft Masonry in all its degrees.

Chapter One

From Darkness to Light

N O MORE needed and useful work is to be done in the Masonic Order today than the education of its members in the true purpose of rites of initiation, that they may the better appreciate the reason, the importance, and the seriousness, of the work the Order was designed to achieve.

Hitherto that educative work has been grievously neglected, with prejudicial results to the Craft through the admission of candidates little adapted to appreciate its purpose. Some members have no wish to be masonically educated. They are content to be Masons in name only, and are satisfied that the monotonous, mechanical repetition of unexplained ceremonies and side-lectures fulfills every requisite, and conveys all that is to be known. Yet in every lodge are to be found brethren who are asking for something more than this, who know that the Craft was designed for wider and better ends; who, as earnest seekers after Wisdom and Light, entered the Order in the hope of finding them, but who too often are repelled by what they do find there, or lose interest when their needs are left unprovided for. It is in the special interest of this worthier type of Mason that this address is given.

We greatly need competent, trained exponents of the meaning and symbolism of the Craft; not merely teachers of the letter of its rituals and lectures. The duty and responsibility of providing this wider instruction surely lies upon those holding the rank of Installed Master. Is not their place in that East from which real Light should continually be coming, and whence they are supposed to employ and instruct in Masonic science those who sit in less or greater degrees of darkness in other symbolic quarters of the lodge? Are they not the figurative representatives of royal Solomon, and symbolic mouthpieces of a more than human wisdom? Over each of them has

there not been raised a most solemn petition that they may be
endued with wisdom to comprehend, judgment to define, and
ability to enforce obedience to the holy law declaring the conditions upon which real initiation depends, so that they may
effectively enlighten the minds of their brethren? How many
Installed Masters are conscious in their hearts of possessing, or
of even striving to acquire, that wisdom, that understanding
of our science, that power of raising others from darkness to
Light in any real and vital sense?

Now you have called me to the presidency of this large
Association of Installed Masters, whose function is to farther
the best interests of the Craft in this district. * In accepting that
position of honor, can I better use it than by inviting you, my
Worshipful Colleagues, to consider with me some lines upon
which true Masonic instruction should be directed, so that we
may combine in raising the general level of Masonic science in
our respective lodges, and at least try to justify more fully our
pretension to be Masters of it?

My purpose now, therefore, is, firstly, to give some idea of
what real initiation involves, and to show how great a difference exists between it and mere formal passage through the
ceremonies of the Craft. Secondly, it is to explain what initiation meant and still means in the more secret and advanced
systems out of which modern Masonry has sprung as a comparatively new branch from a very ancient tree. And lastly, it
is to indicate how, and with what greater efficacy, our lodge-
work might be conducted if we better realized the true nature
and purpose of the Order.

1. Initiation, Real & Ceremonial

It may be a surprise to some members of our Craft to be told
that our ceremonial rites, as at present performed, do not constitute or confer real initiation at all, in the original sense of

* This chapter was originally delivered as the presidential address to the
  Huddersfield and District Installed Masters' Association.—Ed.

admitting a man to the solemn mysteries of the human soul, and to practical experience in divine science. The words "initiation" and "mysteries" have become so popularized and debased that they are nowadays used in relation to familiarizing anyone with the methods of, say, the stock exchange, or any other pursuit with which he is unacquainted.

We profess to confer initiation, but few Masons know what real initiation involves; very few, one fears, would have the wish, the courage, or the willingness to make the necessary sacrifices to attain it if they did. Nevertheless our Craft degrees give us a rough outline and fragmentary sketch of what the real process entails, and they leave it with ourselves either to amplify that sketch by our own efforts and to make its implications such a reality that our whole life becomes transformed in consequence, or to treat it as so much ceremonial through which we are only to pass formally, leaving our old imperfect nature not a whit changed by the process.

Now if Masonry, with its solemn prayers, assurances and pledges, means anything, its true purpose is to promote the spiritual life and development of its members to a degree far in advance of what it accomplishes at present. Otherwise it remains but a social formality, while its obligations and religious references are apt to lapse into profanity or even blasphemy. To prevent this there is needed a dear grasp of the fundamental purpose of an initiatory system and the reason for its existence, after which one can proceed more advantageously to understanding its degrees and symbols in detail. For without such knowledge and understanding there can be no real power, no spiritual driving-force, behind our rites; and without that power ceremonies are but perfunctory, inefficacious formalities. Ceremonies were instituted originally to give an external form to an internal act; but where the internal power to perform such acts does not exist, a ceremony will avail nothing and achieve nothing. You can go on making nominal Masons by the thousand, but you will only be creating a large organization of men who remain as unenlightened in the mysteries as they always were. You cannot make a single real initiate, save, as our teaching indicates, by the help of God and the earnest intelligent cooperation of those qualified to assist to the Light a fellow-being who, from his heart and not merely from his lips, desires that Light, humbly confessing himself spiritually poor, worthless, immersed in darkness, and unable to find that Light elsewhere or by his own efforts. For real initiation means an expansion of consciousness from the human to the divine level.

Every system of real initiation, whether of the past or present, is divided into three clear-cut stages; since before anyone can pass from his natural darkness to the Light supernal and discover the Blazing Star or Glory at his own center, there are three distinct tasks to be achieved. They are as follows: first, the turning away from the attractions of the outer world, involving detachment from the allurements of all that is meant by "money and metals," and the purification and subdual of the bodily and sensual tendencies. Not everyone is able or ripe for doing this; the natural life maintains a powerful hold over us, and our ingrained habits are not readily changed. Yet as long as any of these sensible attractions magnetize and chain us to physical enjoyment, so long are we "in worldly possessions" and precluded from attaining real initiation into what is super-physical. This work of detachment and self-purification is our Entered Apprentice work, and to it, as you know, is theoretically allotted the long period of seven years.*

---

* The reason for the seven years' apprenticeship is based on the septenary principle operating in nature. In the course of each seven years the material particles of the human body become entirely changed and reconstituted. By a course of pure living, diet, and thought for that period, therefore, the physical organism is clarified, sublimated and made a more efficient vehicle for the transmission of the central inner light. This is the true reason for asceticism; the gradual substitution of refined physical tissues for grosser, impure ones.

Second, the analysis, discipline and obtaining control of one's inner world—of the mind, of one's thoughts, one's intellectual and psychic faculties. This extremely difficult task is that of the Fellowcraft stage, to which is allotted a further five years, which with the previous seven make twelve. Because of this, the candidate who had duly completed this period was said, in the ancient systems, to be mystically "twelve years old"—a point to which we will refer again presently.

Third, the "last and greatest trial," lay in the breaking and surrender of the personal will, the dying down of all sense of personality and self-hood, so that the petty personal will may become merged in the divine Universal Will and the illusion of separate independent existence give way to conscious realization of unity with the one Life that permeates the universe. For so only can one be raised from conditions of unreality, strife and figurative death to a knowledge of ultimate reality, peace and life immortal. To attain this is to attain mastership, involving complete domination of the lower nature and the development in oneself of a higher order of life and faculty. And he who thus attained was said to be of the mystical age of thirty years, of which also I will say more presently.

Now it is these three stages, these three labors or processes, that are epitomized dramatically in our three degrees. Every Mason in taking those degrees identifies himself ceremonially with what they signify; he also solemnly obligates himself to put their significance into actual practice in his subsequent life. But it is obvious that those labors are highly arduous tasks demanding the whole time, the persistent thought, and the concentrated energies, of any one who submits himself to them. They are not achieved by merely passing through a sequence of ceremonies in three successive months, at the end of which the candidate, far from being an initiate, usually remains the same bewildered, benighted man he was before, knowing only that he has been hurried through three formal rites entitling him at last to the august title of Master Mason.

Hence we are justified in asserting that Masonry, as now unintelligently practiced, does not and cannot confer real initiation; it merely discharges certain ceremonial formalities. Nevertheless in those formalities the earnest Mason, the diligent pursuer of the path of Light, is given a clear chart of the process of spiritual self-development which he can follow up by his own subsequent exertions; and further, he is directed to a most valuable key for unlocking central truth and discovering the hidden secrets and mysteries of his own being—the key of intense aspiration to find the Light of the center.

"Does that key hang or lie?" asks one of our lectures. * For most Masons it lies. It lies rusting and unused, because they either do not desire or do not know how to use it, or have no one competent to show them how to do so. For some few it hangs—you are taught where—and, though it is of no manner of metal, those who have found and use it, pursuing their quest with fervency and zeal, if perhaps at first with shambling feet and uncertain steps, may assuredly hope to gain admission into the lodge of their own soul, and, when the last hoodwink falls that now blinds their vision, to find themselves there face to face with the Master of that lodge, and in possession of every point of fellowship with Him.

A poet well-schooled in the process of real initiation has thus written of it:

> Pierce thy heart to find the key.
> With thee take
> Only what none else would keep . . .
> Lose, that the lost thou mayst receive;
> Die, for none other way canst live.
> When earth and heaven lay down their veil

---

* This is virtually unknown in American Freemasonry, but it is a very old Masonic tradition, dating to at least the mid-18th century. It is still a part of the Emulation ritual used by most lodges in England. See The Complete Workings of Craft Freemasonry (London: Lewis Masonic, 1982), p. 151.—Ed.

And that apocalypse turns thee pale,
When thy seeing blindeth thee
To what thy fellow-mortals see,
When their sight to thee is sightless,
Their living, death; their light, most lightless;
Seek no more... *

... for it is then, and only then, that true initiation is achieved, that the Lost Word is found at the deep center of one's own heart, and the genuine but withheld secrets of our immortal being are restored to us in exchange for the natural knowledge and faculties which, in this world of time and change, have been given us by Providence as their temporary and mortal substitutions.

2. The Purpose of the Mysteries

We shall understand little of the purpose of Masonry unless we know that of the older systems out of which it issued. That purpose was to promote and expedite the spiritual evolution of those who desired the regeneration of their nature and were prepared to submit to the necessary discipline. Thus the work of the ancient mysteries was something vastly more serious and momentous than merely passing candidates through a series of formal rites as we do today. Their great buildings, which still survive, were assuredly not erected at such immense labor and skill merely to provide convenient meeting-places, like our modern lodge premises, at which to administer a formal rite at the end of a day devoted to business and secular pursuits. The mass of initiation literature and hieroglyphs available to us reveals how drastic and searching was the work to which candidates were subjected under the expert guidance of Masters who had previously undergone the same discipline and become competent to advance their juniors. With them

* From Francis Thompson's poem "The Mistress of Vision" (1913), stanza 20.—Ed.

the work was a difficult but exact science, claiming one's whole time and energies; it was the highest, greatest and holiest of all forms of science—the science of the human soul and the art of its conversion from a natural to a regenerate supernatural state. Reminiscences of the dignity of this work still survive in our references to Masonry as the "noble science" and "royal art," terms meaningless today, although each newly made Mason is charged to make daily progress in Masonic science and every one installed into the chair of a lodge is termed a "Master of Arts and Sciences." [†]

But this secret immemorial science could be imparted only to those morally fit and spiritually ripe for it, as not all men yet are. It was meant only for those bent on passing from the moral and intellectual darkness in which normal humanity is plunged, to that Light which dwells in their darkness, though that darkness comprehendeth it not until it is opened up at their center. It was solely for those who sought the way, the truth and the supernatural life, and were ready to divest themselves of the "money and metals" of temporal interests and concentrate their energies upon the evolution of the higher principles of their nature, which is possible only by the abnegation and surrender of their lower tendencies.

Evolution, nowadays recognized as a universal process in Nature, is sometimes supposed to be a modern discovery. But the ancient wisdom-teaching knew and acted upon it ages before modern scientists discovered it in our own day. It recognized that in all the universe there is but one Life broken up and differentiated into innumerable forms, and evolving through those forms from less to greater degrees of perfection. In Masonic metaphor it saw Nature to be the vast general quarry and forest out of which individual lives have been hewn like so much stones and timber, which when duly perfected are destined to be fitted together and built into a new and higher

† See J. S. M. Ward, *A Complete Ritual of the I. M.* (1921, reprinted London: Lewis Masonic, 1982), p. 20.—Ed.

synthesis, a majestic Temple worthy of the Divine indwelling, and of which Solomon's Temple was a type. All life has issued out of the "East," i.e., from the great world of Infinite Spirit, and has journeyed to the "West" or the little world of finite form and embodiment, whence, when duly perfected by experience in those restricted conditions, it is ordained to return to the "East." Hence when our Entered Apprentice is asked in the lecture, whence he comes and whither he goes, he replies that he is on his way back from the temporal West to the eternal East. The answer corresponds with a fuller one to be found in the surviving records of the early British initiates, the Welsh bards, where to the same question the following reply is made:

> I came from the Great World, having my beginning in Spirit. I am now in the Little World (of form and body) where I have traversed the circle of strife and evolution, and now, at its termination, I am man. In my beginning I had but a bare capacity for life; but I came through every form capable of a body and life to the state of man, where my condition was severe and grievous during the age of ages. I came through every form capable of life, in water, in earth, in air. And there happened to me every severity, every hardship, every. evil, every suffering. But purity and perfection cannot be obtained without seeing and knowing everything, and this is not possible without suffering everything. And there can be no full and perfect Love that does not provide for its creatures the conditions needful to lead to the experience that results in perfection. Every one shall attain to the circle of perfection at last. *

Life, then, was seen as broken up and distributed into innumerable individualized lives or souls and as passing from

---

* From *Barddas*, the ancient initiate tradition of Welsh Druidic Bardism. I have condensed and slightly modernized the wording of the quotation.

one bodily form to another in a perpetual progression. In Masonic metaphor those individualized souls are called "stones," for stone or rock is an emblem of what is most enduring, and the stones are rough ashlars or perfect cubes accordingly as they exist in the rough or have been squared, worked upon, and polished. The bodily form with which the soul becomes invested upon entering this world (symbolized by the Mason being invested with the apron) was seen to be transient, variable, perishable, of small moment compared with the life or soul animating it. Yet it was of the greatest importance in another way, since it provided a fulcrum point or point of resistance for the soul's education and development. It was, as we still term it, the "tomb of transformation"; the grave into which the soul descended for the purpose of working out its own salvation, for transforming and improving itself, and ascending out of it the stronger and wiser for the experience. Thus life was seen as one continuous stream, temporarily checked by the particular form that clothed it, but flowing on from form to form to ever new and higher conditions; slumbering in the mineral, dreaming in the plant, waking in the animal, and reaching moral self consciousness in man.

But does the ascending process end there? Is man as he is now, the goal, the last word, of evolution? Surely, no. As a Persian initiate once wrote:

> I died as a mineral and became a plant.
> I died as a plant and rose to animal.
> I died as an animal and became man.
> Why should I fear? When did I ever grow
>   less by dying?
> Yet once more I shall die as, man, to soar
> With angels blest. But even from angelhood
>   I must pass on.
> I shall become what no mind e'er conceived! †

† Jalaluddin Rumi, "Masnawi."

Now in order that evolution from lower to higher degrees of life may take place, some force must previously have been involved in living organisms that makes their evolution possible. You cannot have evolution without involution. A seed would never grow unless it held within it the force which expands it into a plant with a glory of leaf, flower and fruit. An acorn contains in itself the possibility of the oak. A bird's egg conceals within its fluids the miracle of the feathered bird and the skylark's song. Place any of these in appropriate conditions and the latent life-force will evolve naturally to its preordained limit. The growth may even be artificially accelerated by methods of intensive culture.

What now of man? Man also contains within him a life-force, a "vital and immortal principle" as Masonry calls it,[*] which has not yet expanded to full development in him, and indeed in many men is scarcely active at all. Man, too, has that in him enabling him to evolve from the stage of the mortal animal to a being immortal, superhuman, godlike. Man is evolving towards a far-off divine event in common with all Nature. But how slowly—and how greatly—he thwarts and retards his own development by indulging his gross mortal body and its sensual tendencies, instead of repressing them and cultivating his latent higher principles! Human nature, it is commonly said, continues always the same; its weaknesses and vices are those of thousands of years ago, and looking back over the centuries there is little perceptible improvement in the mass despite our boasted progress and civilization.

Can this long slow process of human evolution be expedited? Is there a method of intensive culture that can be applied to man; one that will more quickly lift him clean above

---

[*] This phrase is not found in most American ceremonies, but in the English Emulation ritual the newly-raised Master Mason is instructed that "even in this perishable frame resides a vital and an immortal principle. . ." See *The Complete Workings of Craft Freemasonry* (London: Lewis Masonic, 1982), p. 119.—Ed.

his present level and transform the sensual, benighted, human animal into an illuminated godlike being?

To this the answer of the ancient mysteries was: "Yes, there is. Human evolution *can* be accelerated; if not at present in the mass of humanity, yet in suitable individuals. Human nature *is* perfectible by an intensive process of purification and initiation. There *is* a royal science of spiritual advancement, and an art of living, by which the latent, undeveloped divine life-principle in man can be liberated from the veils of darkness in him now obscuring it and brought forward into full play. If suitable candidates will but make the requisite sacrifices and submit to the necessary discipline, they can be brought in their present lifetime from darkness to Light; they can be raised to a higher degree of humanity than is otherwise possible to them, and from that position they in turn will be able to raise others to the same degree and so gradually increase the spiritual stature and powers of the whole human race."

The work of the ancient mysteries was, therefore, a "perfecting" work, or a work of initiation introducing men to a new order of life, since it was designed to make imperfect beings whole and perfect by completing their evolutionary possibilities. The Greek word for this, *teleô*, has the twofold meaning "to make perfect" and "to initiate." It occurs constantly in the Scriptures, the greatest textbook of initiation science that exists. They speak of "the just made perfect" (Hebrews 12:23), "be ye perfect as your Father in heaven is perfect" (Matthew 5:48), "we speak wisdom (initiation science) to such as are perfect (or initiated)." (1 Corinthians 2:6) And this perfecting work was for all men alike, of whatever race, language or religion, as Masonry is today. For all are brethren, and upon an equal footing in respect of this work, though not all men are necessarily ready to undertake it at the same moment; all their religions are but so many radii of one circle, designed to lead them from the circumference and surface of life to the one Light at its center.

The qualifications of a candidate for the mysteries were precisely those provided for Masonic candidates today. The one dominant wish of his heart in asking for admission had to be a yearning desire to pass from his natural blindness to the innermost Light, and to have his old imperfect nature revolutionized and transformed. Let me quote one of the oldest prayers in the world, still used in the East by those seeking real initiation. In its original Sanskrit it consists of but six words, which may be Englished thus:

> From the unreal, lead me to the Real!
> From darkness, lead me to Light!
> From the mortal, bring me to Immortality. [*]

It expresses the desire that should be not only upon the lips but burning in the heart of every candidate the world over, under whatever system of initiation he may come. Without that desire as the deepest urge of his heart no real initiation is possible, nor is any candidate properly prepared to ask for it. No one can expect to come to the revelation of the supernatural Light or to be raised to the sublime degree of a master-soul, who is content with his present life as it is, who regards himself as not in darkness but as already enlightened, or supposes his present mortal existence to constitute real life. Only by perceiving the unreality and impermanence of the present world and its interests can one really begin to detach himself from it and divest himself, in thought and desire, of its "money and metals." So long as one carries these with him or remains in any sense "in worldly possessions," so long he darkens his own light and automatically defers his own initiation into it. They mean not merely one's cash and temporal belongings. They include all that clogs and clings to us from our immersion in the outer world; our intellectual possessions, our stores of notions, beliefs and preconceptions about truth, and the mental

[*]   Brihadāranyaka Upanishad 1.3.27.

habits and self-will we have acquired, even with the best motives, in our state of darkness. All these constitute our "worldly
possessions," and they are not our real wealth but our limitations. It is a paradox, but a true one, that we can only gain by
giving them up. Their attraction must cease if that high Light
we profess to seek is ever to be found, and the aspirant for it
must stand at the door of the mysteries in the deepest sense a
poor candidate in a state of darkness, content to be as a child
and surrender himself to an entirely new order and rule of life.
Few are prepared for this task of self-divestment of all that, as
experienced men of the world, they have clung to and built
into their mental fabric. How many of those who ceremonially profess to do so would be ready or content to do it really?
On being told of this prerequisite to initiation they would go
away sorrowful, for they have great possessions, and are not
yet prepared to give them up for something intangible.

In a like sense the candidate had to be a free man; free in
a moral rather than in a civil sense; voluntarily offering himself for the work and free from all attachments hindering its
achievement; and so becoming also free to the goodly fellowship of all other initiates the world over and free from any less
worthy intercourse. He had to be of full age; that is, in full
bodily and mental maturity so as to be fit for the disciplines
awaiting him, and spiritually mature (as not every one is) for
undertaking the final stages of his evolution. Sound judgment,
a sound mind in a sound body, was also essential in view of the
demands made on the mental and psychic faculties, involving
the risk of insanity to the mentally unstable. Strict morals (or
chastity) were imperative, since the task of self-transformation
involves physiological changes in the bodily organism neces-
sitating the utmost personal purity and continence.

And he had to be of good report. This does not mean of
good reputation. It means that on being tested by the initiating authorities he must be found spiritually responsive to the
ideals aimed at and "ring true," giving back a good sound or

report like a coin that is tapped to determine its genuineness. In the wonderful Egyptian rituals in the Book of the Dead, one of the titles always found accorded to the initiate was "true of voice." This is the same thing as our reference to possessing the "tongue of good report." It does not mean that he was incapable of falsity and hypocrisy, which goes without saying, but that his very voice revealed his inherent spirituality and his own speech reflected and was colored by the divine Word behind it. The vocal and heart nervous centers—"the guttural" and "the pectoral," as we say—are intimately related physiologically. Purity or impurity of heart modifies the tonal quality and moral power of one's speech. The voice of the real initiate or saint is always marked by a charm, a music, an impressiveness, and a sincerity absent in other men; for he is "true of voice"; he possesses the "tongue of good report."

The rule of the ancient mysteries was, and still is in other systems, that twelve years of preparation should elapse before the last great spiritual experience was permitted that brought the candidate to the Light at his center and qualified him for Mastership, though less sufficed in appropriate cases. As the result of his purification and labors he had become an illuminate and he was mystically said to be twelve years old. From a rough ashlar he had become a polished perfect cube, a stone meet for building into the "holy city" which we are told lieth foursquare and has twelve gates that are always open. For all the parts of his organism were now equalized and balanced, and all his gates (or channels of intercourse with the divine world), no longer shut and clogged by the darkness of his former impurities, lay open for the passage through them of the true Light. In Masonry, this condition is called the "hour of high twelve"; and he who has attained it will be, like Hiram Abiff, in constant communion with, and adoration of, the Most High.

Similarly, when the candidate had advanced still further to the sublime degree and powers of mastership he was said to be thirty years old. You will find these mystical ages referred to in the third Gospel, where we are told of the Great Exemplar being twelve years old and so illuminated that His wisdom confounded the academic but unenlightened teachers of the Temple (Luke 2:42); and again that He "began to be about thirty years old" (Luke 3:23), at which period began his work as a Master, which continued for another three years and manifested such works and teaching as are possible only to a Master. Thirty-three years was, in the mysteries, the mystical duration of life of every initiate who attained mastership.

That period has no relation to bodily age; it is based on considerations we need not now enter into but referring to the completion of human evolution, when it can be said of the soul's travail:

[It] is finished: He hath wrought the purpose through
Of That which made him man.*

It is for this reason that the Ancient and Accepted Scottish Rite of Masonry extends to 33 degrees, in perpetuation of the original secret tradition.

Of the detailed methods employed in assisting properly qualified candidates to the Light of the center, whether in the ancient systems or at the present day, and of the wonderful change wrought by them in the candidate himself, nothing can be said publicly; these are matters belonging to silence. The secrets and mysteries of real initiation can never be fully communicated except in the course of the process itself. They are not disclosed in Masonry at all. Our teaching refers to them as being "serious, solemn and awful,"† but leaves them at that and provides various substituted ones which have no value save for ceremonial use, and as indications that more genuine ones exist which qualified brethren will come to know when time and

---

* Paraphrased from Sir Edwin Arnold, *The Light of Asia*, book 8, lines 283–284.—Ed.

† Or, in the American work, "wise and serious."—Ed.

circumstances warrant. To all others they will remain sealed. That time and those circumstances depend upon our own desire and efforts. It is an ancient maxim of the science that "when the disciple is ready, the Master will be found waiting" to help on his advancement, and in accordance with this our teaching expressly declares that the purpose of the Mason is to seek a Master and from him to gain instruction. The earnest Masonic disciple whose heart and thought are steadfastly set towards the Light may assuredly count upon finding himself led sooner or later to a real initiate capable of helping him to it and of revealing so much of the real secrets as he is qualified to know.

Real initiates exist at all times, in this country and elsewhere, for the science is not restricted to any nation or creed but is universally diffused over the earth's surface. They are, of course, not numerous and they are to be met with only by those competent to recognize them. They live a hidden life; in the world but not of it. They never seek publicity or honors; they never even disclose the fact that they are initiates. This is the true Masonic secrecy and humility; the greatest among men are content to be as those that are least. The world little suspects what it owes to its hidden initiates.

It would be interesting to say something of them, but time permits of my speaking only of a single case, and I will illustrate the universality of the science by referring (though reticently) to one who is not of our country, color, or creed.

There lives in a distant part of our empire a man who is in the fullest sense a Master Mason. Years ago he embarked upon the great quest of Light, and after the necessary self-preparation under another Master he attained that great spiritual experience which changed his whole nature and raised him finally and permanently from darkness to Light. You may like to know how the daily life of such a man is spent, for it conforms literally with the rule of our symbolic working tool, the 24-inch gauge, in its application to the 24 hours of the day. For at least two hours each day he withdraws entirely from all external affairs, tyling his door as it were against their intrusion, and opens the lodge of his soul to its central depths, passing into blissful, ecstatic communion with the Most High. It is his "hour of high twelve." For another two hours a day he sleeps; that brief period, with a minimum of simple food, sufficing to rest and recuperate his bodily energies, since his real rest and sustenance are drawn from the supernatural peace and bread of life that come to him from his center. The remaining twenty hours of the day are devoted to unflagging labor in the interests of his countrymen and in the spiritual advancement of those brought under his guidance. You may suppose that he is recluse living an unpractical life in a cell or a forest. On the contrary, he is a prominent man who has been knighted for his public service, a King's Counsel, Attorney-General for a large province, a cultured scholar in English and other languages, and the writer of some important books. I have asked British government officials who have worked with him for years whether they have found anything distinctive in him; but they had detected nothing and were utterly blind to the extraordinary spiritual power and saintliness behind his formal exterior. He is one of those who has found, and lives from, the divine center of his being—that point from which a Master Mason cannot err—and accordingly possesses wisdom and powers beyond the imagination of the uninitiated world.

3. The Ideal Lodge

And now, brethren, from what has been said of the ancient and royal science you may see how faithfully our Craft perpetuates the world-old system of elevating men to a higher order of life than they normally experience, and at the same time you may judge how far it falls short in understanding that science and carrying its intentions into practice.

Are we always going to be content with making merely formal Masons and maintaining a merely social and philanthropic society? If so, we shall remain no different men from the popular world who are not Masons. Or are we wishful that the Craft should fulfill its purpose of being a system of real initiating efficiency by awaking the undeveloped spiritual potentialities of its members and raising them to a more sublime level of life? If so, we must educate ourselves more deeply in its meaning.

Let me indicate how things would go if our work were conducted upon more intelligent lines. It is too much to expect any marked or sudden change to take place in old methods or habits, and resistance to any improvement may always be expected from some who are satisfied with things as they are. Nor can improvement be forced upon anyone; to be advantageous it must come spontaneously. But many brethren and many lodges sincerely desire it, and so let me offer you a picture of what an ideal lodge would be; you may then consider how far it may be practicable to attempt to conform to that ideal.

In the first place, lodge meetings would be primarily devoted to what we are taught is their chief purpose, namely, to expatiating on the mysteries of the Craft and educating brethren in the understanding of them. This is now never done; largely because we are without competent instructors. We suppose that our side-lectures are sufficient instruction. This is not the case. There are additional large fields of knowledge that Masons must explore if they wish to learn this science, while our official lectures are themselves packed with purposely obscured truths that are left to our own efforts and perspicuity to discover, but the purport of which at present remains entirely concealed.

The duly opened lodge would be a sanctuary of silence and contemplation, broken only by ceremonial utterances or such words of competent and luminous instruction as the Master or Past Masters are moved to extend. And the higher the degree in which it is opened, the deeper and more solemn would be the sense of excluding all temporal thoughts and interests and of approaching more nearly that veiled central Light whose opening into activity in our hearts we profess to be our predominant wish.

In such circumstances each lodge meeting would become an occasion of profound spiritual experience. No member would wish to disturb the harmony of such a lodge by talk or alien thought. No member would willingly be absent. If he were, save from necessity, it would indicate that, though entitled to wear the apron in a literal sense, he was temporarily not properly clothed in his mind and intention to be qualified to enter the lodge. Every one would regret when such a meeting closed and it became necessary to be recalled from such peace and refreshment to the jars and labors of the outer world.

The admission of a new candidate would be a comparatively infrequent event. For no one would be received to membership save after the fullest tests of his genuine desire for Masonic knowledge and of his adaptability to it. The conferment of the different degrees would be at much longer intervals than is now authorized, so as to ensure their being assimilated and understood, as is impossible at present. And upon the notable occasion of a degree being conferred, those present would be not merely passive spectators of the rite. They would have been educated to become active though silent helpers in it by adding the force of their united thought and desire to the spoken word, and so creating such a tense and highly charged atmosphere that an abiding permanent uplift in the candidate's consciousness might be hoped for. For the efficacy of rites like ours does not depend solely on the Master who performs them. He is the mouthpiece for the time being of all those present, but it is the whole assembly that should really be acting; forming, as it were, a battery of spiritual energy, and drawing the new brother into vital fraternity with itself. Great power resides in strong collective thought and intention, and when these are focused and concentrated upon a candidate properly prepared in heart and mind for our ministrations, we might hope to induce in him something like real initiation; but otherwise he will be listening to but a formal recital of words.

It follows that we should never hear such things as the usual talk about "making one's lodge a success," or as personal praise to anyone for having performed his work creditably. Whether our work is really done well, in the sense of being spiritually effective, God alone knoweth, to whom all gratitude should be rendered for any good achieved; while the only worthy success for a lodge is its capacity for vitally affecting the lives of those who enter it and transforming their mental and moral outlook.

The lodge-room should be holy ground, a Temple consecrated to Masonic work and used for it exclusively. For it is a symbol of the temple of the human individual, and we who are taught the necessity of every intending initiate's excluding money and metals from his thought, and who have before us the significant example of a Master who vigorously scourged all money-changers out of the Temple, should surely conform to those lessons by keeping our symbolic temple sanctified and entirely free from secular use. There is a practical advantage in so doing, for premises continually devoted to a single purpose become, as it were, charged and saturated with the thought and ideals thrown off by those who habitually so use it. A permanent spiritual atmosphere is created, the influence of which appreciably affects those who enter it, and the possibility of the efficacious initiation of candidates is thereby greatly increased; whereas that atmosphere becomes defiled, and any spiritual influence stored in it neutralized, by promiscuous use.

Visiting other lodges would no longer be for social reasons, but, as in ancient times, solely with a desire to enlarge one's Masonic knowledge and experience, to share their spiritual privileges, or even to bring spiritual reinforcement to lodges needing such help. No practice is more beneficial than intercourse between those of different lodges engaged in a

common work, and no right is more firmly established than
that of any seeker of the Light to claim and be given hospitality
and assistance conducing to that end. But our modern practice of mass-visiting is calculated to disturb the true work we
ought to be doing, and is somewhat of an abuse and travesty
of a privilege dating from antiquity, when occasional representatives of one school of the mysteries journeyed, often long
distances, to another in a different land to enlarge their own
knowledge or impart it to those they visited.*

Promotion to office in the Craft would not be by rota-
tion or from seniority of membership or social standing in the
outside world. It would depend entirely upon spiritual proficiency; upon ability to impart real illumination to candidates
and advance the true work of the Craft. The little jealousies
and heart-burnings that now occur at the annual promotions
would be impossible; such things belong to the base metals
in our nature, which ought long ago to have been got rid of
in any one really qualified for office. Did we better realize the
serious nature of initiation work, we should often shrink in
humility from accepting positions we are now eager to seize.
Remember that in leaving the outer world and. passing the
portal of the lodge into the world within, all values change;
all questions, and even all sense, of personality should cease.
You become engaged not in a personal task but in a common
fraternal work before God, in whose sight all are equal and
who will act through such instruments as seem good to Him.
Therefore "let him that is greatest among you be as he that is
least"—it may well be that the apparently least among us is
often likely to be the more efficient workman.

---

*   The ancient pagan mysteries were famous for borrowing from one
     another, and Philo of Alexandria, representing the Jewish mysteries,
     enjoined his readers: "And if ever you meet with anyone who has been
     properly initiated, cling to that man affectionately and adhere to him,
     that if he has learned any more recent mystery he may not conceal it
     from you before you have learned to comprehend it thoroughly." (On
     the Cherubim § 48)—Ed.

These, I know, are lofty ideals, largely impracticable at the. moment, and I have no wish to alienate any Brother's interest in the Craft by imposing a standard beyond his present capacity and desire. Yet brethren to whom the ideal appeals, and to whom it is both desirable and practicable, might unite in meeting with the intention of conforming to it, and here and there even a small new lodge might be formed for that special purpose, leaving other lodges to work on their accustomed lines.

Is Masonry, throughout, anything but a lofty ideal, which so far we have made little serious attempt to realize? The main difficulty before us is that the true work of the Craft contemplates a much greater detachment from the things and the ways of the outer world than we are at present willing, or perhaps able, to allow. So we compromise with ourselves, and seek to combine the outer secular life with the inner ideals of the Craft. The two conflict, and no man can efficiently serve two masters. We must choose whom we will serve.

Still the ideal is before us, a glimmering light in a dark, distracted and dying world, and it rests with ourselves whether it remains a glimmer or whether we strive to fan it into a blaze of fact. For those who desire merely a social and sociable organization, garnished with a little picturesque ceremonial and providing opportunity for a little amusement and personal distinction, Masonry will never be more than the formality it long has been and still is for many, and they themselves will remain in darkness as to its meaning, its purpose, and its great possibilities.

But for those who are not content with vanities and unrealities, who desire not a formal husk but the living spirit, and are bent on plumbing its well-guarded secrets and mysteries to their depth and living out its implications to the full, Masonry may well come—as for some it has come—to be the chief blessing and experience of their lives; it may yield them even the last secret of life itself. It may fulfill for them the ancient prayer of the Eastern initiates we just now spoke of, by leading them from the unreal to the supreme Reality, from darkness to Light ineffable, from the things of time and mortality to things immortal. They may find it a ladder of truth and world-escape set up for them in the wilderness around them, and their lodge a place of unfolding vision where, with the Hebrew patriarch, they will exclaim: "This is none other than a house of God and a gate of heaven!" (Genesis 28:17)

Chapter Two
Light on the Way

They went up with winding stairs
into the middle chamber,
   and out of the middle into the third.—1 Kings 6:8

"Does the road wind up-hill all the way?"
  Yes, to the very end.
"Will the day's journey take the
    whole long day?"
  From morn to night, my friend!
"But is there for the night a resting-place?
  A roof for when the slow dark hours begin?
  May not the darkness hide it from my face?"
    You cannot miss that Inn. — Christina Rossetti

IN the previous paper we have spoken of the transition from darkness to light made by those who seek to effect the reconstitution of their natural being and to develop it, by the science and methods of initiation, to a higher and ultra-natural level.

It has been made clear that that transition must necessarily be gradual, and that, though ceremonially dramatized in three degrees which can be taken in successive months, to realize the implications of those degrees in actual life-experience may be a lifetime's work; perhaps more than a lifetime's. The Apprentice who has entered himself to the business of rebuilding his own soul has much to learn and to do before he becomes even a competent Craftsman in it; the Craftsman, in turn, has much to do and far to journey before he can hope for complete mastership. The work of self-transmutation is a strenuous one, not suddenly or hurriedly to be performed, and one needing hours of refreshment and passivity as well as hours of active labor, to each of which he will find himself duly summoned at the proper time. There is much to be learned in regard to the secrets of his own nature and the principles of intellectual science, which only gradually, and as the result of patience and experience, can become revealed to his view. There is a superstructure to be raised, perfect in all its parts; a work involving much more than is at first supposed. There are tests and ordeals of a searching character to be undergone on the way.

A measure of Light, a first glimpse of the distant Promised Land, may come to the eager sight of the properly prepared candidate from the first moment of his entrance upon the work, but he must not suppose that he has yet fully captured it and made it permanently his own. It is something, however, to have felt that a veil has been suddenly withdrawn from his previously darkened sight and that he has become able to distinguish between his former benightedness and the goal lying before him.

We will entitle this present section, therefore, "Light on the Way," and make it treat of a variety of matters calling for the aspirant's attention as he pursues the way that intervenes between his first glimpse of the Light and its ultimate realization; and in a subsequent section we shall speak of Light in its fullness of attainment. We will supplement our previous explanation of Masonic doctrine by dealing with further symbols and passages in the rituals, with which every Mason is familiar formally and by the outward ear, but the significance of which too often passes unexplained and unobserved.

The expositions in this section are offered not only for the private reflection of members of the Craft, but with the suggestion that they may serve the as material for collective meditation by brethren in open lodge or at Lodges of Instruction. For those upon the path to real initiation, meditation is essential. For meditation opens a window in the mind through which Light streams into the understanding from the higher, spiritual principle in ourselves; which window is symbolized by the dormer-window in the emblematic Temple of Solo-

mon,* through which came light to those ascending the stairway that wound inwardly to the middle chamber, and leading
to the central sanctuary where alone Light in its fullness was
to be found.†

The practice of meditation, moreover, whether personal
or collective, conduces to that quietness and control of the
normally restless, wandering mind. which are indispensable
for the apprehension of deep truth. Ancient lodges, we are
told, were wont to meet on the highest hills and in the lowest valleys; and in an old instruction-lecture it is explained
that those expressions are meant to be figurative and relate
less to actual places than to the spiritual and mental condition of those assembled. To meet in the valley, implied being in a state of sheltered passiveness and tranquility, when
the minds of the brethren surrendered themselves to quiet
collective thought on the subject of their work; and thus, being "led beside still waters," they became, like the limpid un-
ruffled surface of a lake, a clear undistorting mirror for the
reflection and apprehension of such rays of light and truth as
might reach them from above. To meet on the high hills, on
the other hand, implied the more active work of the lodge and
the performance of it upon the supra-physical planes—the
"hills" of the spirit; for the real work of initiation is only there
accomplished, and is no longer a ceremonial formality.

*   The dormer window was a common symbol in early Freemasonry,
     still retained in the English Emulation Rite, but not found in most
     American Masonic traditions. "The ornaments of a Master Mason's
     Lodge are the Porch, Dormer, and Square Pavement. The porch was
     the entrance to the *Sanctum Sanctorum*, the Dormer, the window that
     gave light to the same, and the Square Pavement for the High Priest to
     walk on." See *The Complete Workings of Craft Freemasonry* (Lewis Masonic,
     1982), p. 127. The dormer window was likely removed from some
     rituals because no such window existed in the historical Temple of
     Solomon, but its esoteric symbolism is still valuable. —Ed.

†   In monastic orders the equivalent of the dormer-window is the
     tonsure or shaven top of the priest's head, through which Light from
     above may be thought of as descending into the mind.

There are times for work and times for repose in the Craftsman's task—times of labor and refreshment—and to perform that task efficiently both must be utilized. Modern lodges, in the general imperfect conception of Masonry, follow merely the rush and hustle methods of the outside world, which, of course, inside the lodge have no place and ought no longer to be emulated. They are busy enough on the active side, but they provide no opportunity for cultivating the equally necessary passive aspect of the work. It would be found eminently advantageous, therefore, if lodges which desire to realize true Masonry adopted the practice of collectively contemplating points of symbolism and teaching; devoting certain meetings to this special purpose, and then, without more discussion than is necessary and helpful, quietly and earnestly concentrating attention upon the significance of some symbol or point of doctrine brought before them.

For those seriously engaged in the ascent of the winding staircase, the following expositions may perhaps serve as helpful rays of light from the dormer-window. They are necessarily brief and merely elementary introductions to phases of the science which, as the aspirant proceeds, he will find inexhaustible and claiming not cursory notice but his constant deep attention. May they, however, be as a lamp to his feet and a light upon the spiral path to ledge his own middle chamber, and help to guide him to that final central sanctuary where the Light itself shines in fullness and waits to be found.

1. "The Knowledge of Yourself"

It has already been shown that the structure and appointments of the lodge are symbolic; that the lodge is a representation both of the universe and of man himself as a Microcosm or the universe in miniature; that it is an image of his own complex constitution, his heavens and his earth (his spirituality and materiality) and all that therein is.

By contemplating that image, therefore, the Mason learns to visualize himself; he is given a first lesson in that self-knowledge in the full attainment of which is promised the understanding of all things. "Know thyself," we have said, was written over the portals of the ancient temples of initiation, self-knowledge being the aim of their intention and the goal of their purpose. Masonry perpetuates this maxim by recommending self-knowledge as "the most interesting of all human studies." It is the tersest, wisest of instructions, yet little heeded nowadays, and it is incapable of fulfillment unless undertaken in accordance with the ancient science and with a concentration of one's whole energies upon the task.

It involves the deepest introspection into oneself and perfect discrimination between what is real and permanent, and what is unreal and evanescent in ourselves. As aspirants to the mysteries could not learn the secrets of the temple without entering it, learning its lessons, undergoing its disciplines, and receiving its graduated initiations, so no one can attain self-knowledge save by entering into himself, distinguishing the false from the true, the unreal from the real, the base metal from the fine gold, sublimating the former into the latter, and ignoring what is negligible or superfluous. The very word initiation primarily derives from the Latin inire, to go within; and thence, after learning the lessons of self-analysis, to make a new beginning (initium) by reconstructing one's knowledge of life and manner of living. The 43rd Psalm restates the same instruction: Introibo ad altare Dei, "I will go in to the divine altar."[*] Similarly, the Masonic initiation contemplates a going within oneself, until one reaches the altar or center, the Divine Principle or ultimate hidden basis of our being.

To know the anatomy and physiology of the mortal body is not self-knowledge. The physical fabric of man is a perishing self, mere dust and shadow, projected from vitalizing forces within it, and without permanence or reality.

* Cited from the Latin Vulgate's version of Psalms 43:4.—Ed.

To understand the nature and mechanism of the mind, emotions and desires, is useful and necessary, but is not self-knowledge, for they, too, are transient and, therefore, unreal aspects of the deeper real self. The personality we present to the world is not our real self. It is but a mask, a distorting veil, behind which the true self abides hiddenly and often unknown to our unreal surface self, unless and until it be brought forward into consciousness, displacing and overriding the notions and tendencies of the natural, but benighted, superficial self. Until then its "light shineth in darkness and the darkness comprehendeth it not." (John 1:5) To bring it forward out of its veils of darkness, to "comprehend" and establish it permanently in our awareness is, and has ever been, the purpose of all initiation. But this cannot be achieved until the outer bodily and mental vestures have been purified and a voluntary dying or effacement of everything in us alien to, or conflicting with, the real self has been suffered; all which is implied by the teaching of our three degrees respectively.

True self-knowledge is *unobstructed conscious union of the human spirit with God and the realization of their identity.* In that identic union the unreal, superficial selves have become obliterated. The sense of personality is lost, merged in the impersonal and universal. The little ego is assumed into the great All, and knows as It knows. Man realizes his own inherent ultimate divinity, and thenceforth lives and acts no longer as a separate individual, with an independent will, but in integration with the Divine Life and Will, whose instrument he becomes, whose purposes he thenceforth serves.

This is "the great day of atonement," when the limited personal consciousness becomes identified or made at one with one's own divine, omniscient, vital and immortal principle, which each must realize as the high priest of his personal temple and after many washings and purifications against the contrary tendencies of his former unregenerate nature. This was the secret supreme attainment hinted at in the cryptic maxim "Know thyself!" Each of us may judge for himself whether he has yet reached it.

To find our own center, our real self, involves, therefore, a turning inwards of our previously externalized faculties of sense and thought, and an introspective penetration of the outlying circumferential elements of our nature until the "center" is found. This task is figured by our ceremonial per-ambulations and by the path of the winding staircase leading from the ante-rooms and forecourts of our nature to the center, up which the aspirant must ascend, asking, seeking, knock-ing, all the way; being subjected from time to time to tests of his progress and receiving, without scruple or diffidence, such wages of good fortune or adversity as unseen Providences may know to be his due.

The inmost sanctuary he will find closely guarded. Noth-ing unclean can enter or approach that holy place. Hence in the biblical description of the symbolic Temple one finds that, in the forecourt, stood the great laver of water for the cleansing of pollutions, and the altar of fire for the sacrificial burning up of one's impurities. The sword of the Inner Guard,* directed to those unqualified to enter the lodge, is the Masonic way of inculcating that peril exists to those who are not properly pre-pared to approach the Center or who would "rush in where angels fear to tread"†; it corresponds with the sword of the Cherubim in Genesis, which turned every way to keep the way to the Tree of Life from the approaches of the unfit.

Mental as well as physical purity is indispensable to real initiation, but is far more difficult of the two to acquire. Modern psychology discloses not only how fractional a part

---

* American Freemasons may be unfamiliar with the Inner Guard, an officer in English lodges who is the counterpart to the Tyler or Outer Guard, and who performs duties that are assigned to either the Senior or Junior Deacons in most of the Masonic jurisdictions of the United States.—Ed.

† This famous saying was minted in 1711 by poet and Freemason, Alexander Pope, in *An Essay on Criticism*, line 625.—Ed.

of our entire mentality functions above the threshold of our
normal awareness, but also what knots and twists, what mental lumber, what latent horrors and accumulations of inner
foulness, lie stored in the subconsciousness of even those living ordinarily clean lives. They are the deposits of the mind's
past activities; forgotten often by the conscious mind itself,
yet automatically registered upon our impalpable mind-stuff
by the recording pencil (mentioned among the third degree
working-tools) which at every moment of our lives posts up
entries of our thoughts, words, and actions. For at the center of
ourselves is the All-observant Eye; so that we ourselves constitute our own judgment book, wherein each of us unwittingly
inscribes his own history and formulates his own destiny, and
its pages we have each to read ourselves.

With these mental deposits and consolidations those
skilled in initiation science are well familiar. The modern psychologist calls them "complexes." In the old treatises on the subject they are termed foul ethers, congelations of impure mental
matter. They are the "base metals" of Masonry. Each of us has
been an artificer of those metals and worked them into all man-
ners of grotesque designs in his mental nature, and hence the
conferment upon the candidate, at a certain stage, of a name
attributed to the first of such artificers and signifying him to
be still incompletely purged of worldly possessions of this kind.
These "base metals" require to be discharged from the system
by a long process of corrective purifying thought and aspiration and to be transmuted into gold, or pure mind-stuff, before
real initiation is possible. No inward fog must intervene between the outer and innermost organs of consciousness when
the time comes for these to be unified. The light of truth cannot
penetrate a mind crammed with pernicious thought and with
opinions to which it clings tenaciously. It must empty itself of
all preacquired knowledge and prejudices, and then rise on the
wings of its own genius into the realm of independent thought
and there learn Truth at first hand by directly beholding it.

The incident of attaining Light and self-knowledge is dramatically emphasized in Masonic ceremonial. It is represented by that important moment in the ritual of the third degree when darkness suddenly gives way to bewildering light, in which light the candidate gazes back for the first time upon the remains of his own past and beholds the emblems of his own mortality.* He has now (at least in ceremony) surmounted the great transitional crisis involved in becoming raised from a natural to a higher order of humanity. He perceives his temporal organism to have been the "tomb of transformation," in which the great change has been wrought. He has risen from that tomb, and for him the old grave of the natural body has lost its sting, and that spiritual unconsciousness, which is termed "death," has been swallowed up in the victory won at last by his higher eternal principle over his lower temporal one. The mystical sprig of acacia has bloomed at the head of his grave, by the efflorescence of the vital and immortal principle in his purified mind and neural system.

Thus is portrayed for us, in Masonic ceremony, the moment of attainment of knowledge of one's true self. The incident, let it be emphasized, does not involve the physical death of the body and its faculties, for to "the companions of his former toils"† the purified mind will thereafter be reunited. But thenceforth they will be his docile, plastic, obedient servants, and no longer his master. He will continue to live in the world for the remainder of his appointed span, no longer for his own sake, but for the uplifting and advancement of his fellowmen to his own high degree. His expansion of consciousness and wisdom will become part of his equipment for practical work

* It is again portrayed, with much more elaborate detail, in the climax of the Royal Arch degree ceremony, as I have described in my previous volume (The Meaning of Masonry).

† In the British Emulation Rite, Master Masons are said to be raised "from a figurative death to a union with the former companions of their toils." See The Complete Workings of Craft Freemasonry (Lewis Masonic, 1982), p. 282.—Ed.

in the world. His own spiritual evolution is complete, so far as the educative experience of this world can take it; he lives now to help on that of humanity.

A great and good brother, reviewing his long connection with Masonic sanctuaries more than a century ago, wrote thus about initiation:

> The only initiation which I preach and seek with all the ardour of my soul, is that by which we may enter into the heart of God, and make God's heart enter into us, there to form an indissoluble marriage, which will make us the friend, brother and spouse of our divine Redeemer."[‡]

This attainment is the self-knowledge pointed to by the Craft teaching, and to which that teaching seeks to guide the reflections of every Masonic initiation has no other end than this—conscious union between the individual soul and the Universal Divine Spirit.

This union is symbolized by the familiar conjunction of the square and the compasses. The square is the emblem of the soul; the compasses of the spirit which indwells in that soul. At first the Mason sees the points of the compasses concealed behind the square, and, as he progresses, their points emerge from that concealment until both become superimposed upon the square. Thus is indicated the progressive subordination of the soul and the corresponding coming forward of the ultimate spirit into personal consciousness, so that the Mason can "work with both those points," thus becoming an efficient builder in the spirit and rendering the circle of his own being complete by attaining conscious alliance with his ultimate and only true self.

---

‡ Letter from Louis Claude de Saint Martin to Baron de Liebistorf Kirchberger, dated 19 June 1797, and reproduced in E.B. Penny (Ed.), *Theosophic Correspondence* (William Roberts, 1863), p. 374. Wilmshurst calls this "a work of great value and disclosing the nature of Masonic work in French lodges prior to the Revolution of 1789."—Ed.

2. The Letter "G"

Centrally, in the ceiling of each lodge, is exhibited this striking symbol.* It is the emblem of the Divine Presence in the lodge; it is also the emblem of that Presence at the spiritual center of the individual Mason. Its correspondence in the Christian church is the perpetual light burning before the high altar.

In the first and second Craft degrees the symbol is visible in the heavens of lodge. In the third degree it has become invisible, but its presence is still manifested, being reflected in the small light in the East which, in correspondence with the Divine Presence is—as every Mason knows—inextinguishable even in one's darkest moments. In the Royal Arch degree it again becomes visible, but in another form and in another position—on the floor of the Temple and at its center, and in the form of a cubical altar, a white stone, bearing the Sacred Name. In the course of the degrees, therefore, it has come down from heaven to earth; Spirit has descended to the plane of purified Matter; the Divine and the human have been brought together and made one. God has become Man; Man has been unified with God, and has found the Divine Name written upon the altar of his own heart.

In the significance of this symbol and its transpositions during the four degrees may, therefore, be discerned the whole purpose and end of initiation, the union of the personal soul with its Divine Principle. Masonry has no other objective than this; all other matters of interest connected with it are but details subsidiary to this supreme achievement.

When the lodge is opened, the mind and heart of every brother composing it should be deemed as also being opened to the "G" and all that it implies, to the intent that those implications may eventually become realized facts of experience. When the lodge is closed, the memory of the "G" symbol and

---

* In English lodges, the letter G is typically either on or suspended from the center of the ceiling of the lodge. In American lodges, it is displayed above the Master's station in the symbolic East.—Ed.

its implications should be the chief one to be retained and pondered over in the repository of the heart.

Further, great significance lies in the centrality of the "G." The lodge is grouped around it, not assembled immediately below it. It is as though this Blazing Star or Glory in the cen-ter[†] burned with too fierce a light for anything less pure and bright than itself to withstand the descent of its direct rays; and, accordingly, the floor of the lodge is left open and unoc-cupied; and only at its extremities do the assembled brethren sit, removed from its direct rays. Directly beneath it lies the checker-work floor; the symbol of the manifested creation, where the one White Light from above becomes differenti-ated into perpetual duality and opposites of light and dark-ness, good and evil, positive and negative, male and female, as evidenced by the black and white squares, yet the whole held together in a unity as is denoted by the symbolic skirt-work around the same.

The "G" therefore denotes the Universal Spirit of God, permeating and unifying all things. It is a substitute for the Hebrew letter Yod, the tenth letter of the Hebrew alphabet, and out of which all the other letters of that alphabet are con-structed in correspondence with the truth that all created things are modifications of the one primal Spirit.

In the instruction lecture of a degree outside our present constitutions, the "G" is explained as having a three-fold refer-ence; (1) the Glory of God, or glory in the center; (2) Grandeur, or the greatness of perfection to which man may become raised by initiation into union with God at his center; (3) Gom-El, a Hebrew word of praise for the Divine power and goodness in

† The letter G was originally associated with the symbol of the Blazing Star, rather than the Square and Compass. Wilmshurst refers to the old traditions preserved in the British Emulation Rite, which teaches that "the Blazing Star, or Glory in the center, refers us to the Sun, which enlightens the earth," and also that "the Sun, the Glory of the Lord, rises in the East and sets in the West." See *The Complete Workings of Craft Freemasonry* (Lewis Masonic, 1982), p. 180 & 190.—Ed.

designing that perfection and that union between the Creator and the creature. There is also a Hebrew tradition that *Gom-El* was the word uttered by Adam on first beholding the beauty of Eve and perceiving the ultimate destiny of humanity.*

The "G" had its equivalent in the Egyptian mysteries in the solar symbol of Ra, the spiritual Sun. In the great temple of the Greek mysteries at Delphi, where the Eleusinian initiations took place for seventeen centuries, it was represented by the fifth letter of the Greek alphabet, the E (or *epsilon*); five being a numerical symbol of man in the Pythagorean system, as evidenced by his five senses, the five-fold extension of his hands and feet, and in accordance with considerations of a more abstruse nature.† Hence the five-pointed star (or pentagram) is also a symbol of man, and expresses a variety of truths concerning him. In the rituals in the *Book of the Dead* the candidate is described as a "keeper of five"; operative fellow-craft masons worked in batches of five, and a speculative Fellowcraft lodge today consists of five brethren; all these allusions having a deeper significance than can be explained here, but bearing upon the present state of human evolutionary development.

Plutarch records that the "E" was regarded as a symbol of the greatest importance and instructiveness and was exhibited in three forms (corresponding with our three degrees), first

---

* Wilmshurst here refers to the three interpretations of the letter G as given in some versions of the Secret Master degree, the 4° of the Ancient and Accepted Scottish Rite. Wilmshurst's suggestion of a Hebrew tradition about *gomel* being Adam's first word is apparently erroneous, and the word *gomel* does not imply, as the author writes, a "union between the Creator and the creature." The Scottish Rite tradition may have originated in the idea that upon first seeing Eve, Adam recited a common prayer of thanksgiving called *birkat ha-gomel* ("the blessing of Him who bestows").—Ed.

† While the Greek letter E was in fact suspended between two pillars at Delphi, the Eleusinian mysteries were celebrated in Eleusis only and never at Delphi. Also, it should be noted that in the original edition, Wilmshurst confused the *êta* (which is H, the eighth Greek letter) with the *epsilon* (E, the fifth letter). The current edition corrects this.—Ed.

in wood, afterwards in bronze, and finally in gold.[‡] The progression signified a corresponding advance of the candidate's moral and spiritual nature under the discipline of initiation. He is likened at first to soft, perishable wood; hardening into the durability of bronze; which impure, alloyed metal finally becomes sublimated into gold—the symbol of the attainment of purity, wisdom and perfection to which initiation leads.

Beyond this, however, the central symbol had another deep meaning. The great initiation-temples of antiquity, as also certain Christian churches of historic interest (such as those of Iona and Glastonbury, from which Britain became Christianized), were erected at certain focal points of the earth's surface known to the initiates of the time as being magnetic centers or nodal points of spiritual force peculiarly favorable for the influx into this world of currents of divine power and for their irradiation thence to surrounding regions. Each such place was called an *omphalos*, a navel, or mystical center; and the Temple at Delphi is related to have been built where it was under divine guidance and for that purpose; and we know that it became the center of light and religion to the then civilized Western world for seventeen centuries.

This historical fact and this occult principle are now reproduced in Masonry. Every lodge, every place of initiation, is in theory—though not nowadays in practice—held at a center or physical focus-point selected as being favorable both to the initiation of those who enter it and to the spiritual advancement of the uninitiated popular world resident in its vicinity. "A city set on a hill cannot be hid." (Matthew 5:14) A Temple or lodge of brethren intelligently performing its work is not only engaged in a work of spiritual building as regards its own members; it is, though perhaps unconsciously, at the same time, generating and throwing off vibrations of spiritual energy to all around it; its occult influence extends, and its radiations are of efficacy, to a greater range than one dreams of.

‡   Plutarch, Moralia 385F – 386A.

If, then, the lodge be a spiritual focus-point, the center of the lodge, where the "G" is exhibited, is its most vital and sacred point; the point at which Divine Energy may be thought of as concentrated and specially powerful. And the reason will become clear for placing the candidate at that point at a certain moment in the Ceremony.

Why is he then placed in the center? Previously he has been placed, not there, but in certain more removed places in the lodge; in the Northeast or the Southeast corners where the intensity of the central Light is theoretically less powerful, where it is tempered and adjusted to his as yet unperfected organism, and where charges and instruction appropriate to his then state of advancement are imparted to him. But when directed to be placed in the lodge-center, he is called upon to stand, as it were, in direct alignment with the descending ray of the Supernal Light and to bear the stress of its full current. The intensity of that current can only be borne and withstood by one who is perfect in all his parts and in whom the sensual, emotional, and mental natures have been purified, rectified and brought into harmony and to an alignment corresponding with the physical and moral erectness of a just and upright man; an unpurified man would run the peril of having his organism injured or shattered by a current of that fiery Power, by which every soul must sooner or later be tested, but which consumes everything not assimilable with itself. The three Hebrew "children" (i.e., initiates) who withstood unscathed the fiery furnace into which they were plunged, typify the truth here testified to. (Daniel 3:19-27)

When, therefore, a candidate is placed in the center of the lodge, beneath the "G" symbol, let those assembled around him try to realize the intention of what is thereby implied.* Let them reflect that at that important moment, more perhaps

---

* American Freemasons will remember that the symbolic Center of the Lodge is identified with the Blazing Star. While the letter G has been relocated to the East, the Blazing Star remains in the location Wilmshurst describes, and so the American and British work are in harmony, though somewhat different in outer form.—Ed.

LIGHT ON THE WAY

than at any other in the ceremonies, it is possible for the celestial Light to descend upon the duly prepared candidate, to flood his heart and expand his mind, and so to open his understanding to the instruction then communicated to him that he may realize the spirit as well as hear the letter of it, while standing in that sacred position. And let them at that moment silently and earnestly invoke the Light of the Center, that it may then consciously arise in both him and them, so that what is done ceremonially may become for them both, a great fact of spiritual experience.

The point is emphasized here with earnestness, because the Masonic procedure of placing the candidate in the center of the lodge at an important stage of his progress not only perpetuates a traditional and purposeful ancient practice, but also accords with what occurs in initiations of a much more advanced and real character than it is possible to speak of here, as those who become duly qualified will one day come to find. By understanding and being faithful in the small things of even an elementary and ceremonial system, one becomes educated for and prepared to be entrusted with greater ones when the time for acquiring them arrives.

3. The Ladder

A most important part of the curriculum of the ancient mysteries was instruction in cosmology, the science of the universe. The intention of that instruction was to disclose to candidates the physical and metaphysical constitution of the world and the place and destiny of man in it. They were shown how the complex human organism reproduces the great world and summarizes it in small, so that man may see himself to be a microcosm or miniature copy of it. They were enlightened not only upon the external visible aspect, but also upon the physically unseen and impalpable aspect, both of the universe and themselves. They learned truths concerning the material and the ultra-material sides of the world and were taught that corresponding features were present in themselves. They learned of the continual flux of matter, of the transiency of bodily forms, and of the abiding permanence of the one life or spirit which has descended and embodied itself in matter, and has there distributed and clothed itself in an endless but progressive variety of forms from the mineral up to the human, with the purpose of generating eventually a finished perfected product as the result of the mighty process. There was demonstrated to them the dual cosmic method of involution and evolution, by which the universally diffused life-force involves and circumscribes itself within material limitations and physical conditions, and thence evolves and arises out of them, enriched by the experience. They were taught of the different levels and graduations of the universe—some of them material and some ethereal—the planes and sub-planes of it, upon which the great scheme is being carried out; which levels and planes, all progressively linked together, constitute as it were one vast ladder of many rounds, staves, or rungs; a ladder which Tennyson once well described as

> The world's great altar-stairs
> Which slope through darkness up to God.[*]

Candidates in the old systems were instructed in these matters before being admitted to initiation. The knowledge served to explain to them their own nature and constitution and their place in the world-system. It demonstrated to them their own evolutionary possibilities and made clear to them why initiation science had been instituted, and how initiation itself was an intensive means of accelerating the spiritual evolution of individuals who were ripe for it, and capable of intelligently cooperating with and expediting the cosmic process. With this knowledge they were then free either to proceed to actual initiation and undertake its obligations, sacrifices and

[*]   "In Memoriam A.H.H." (1859), chapter 55, lines 15–16.

discipline, or to stand down and go no farther if they found themselves unwilling, or without the courage, to undertake the arduous task involved. Freedom of the personal will in this momentous choice was always essential to admission to initiation, and the same absence of constraint still attaches to admission to modern Masonry.

The modern Mason, however, is left entirely without any cosmological instruction and to such hazy notions on the subject as he may happen to hold. It becomes difficult, therefore, in regard to this and many other matters of Masonic moment, to speak of the *disciplina arcani* to those who may be either not interested in it or who would treat the information with incredulity as something about which nothing certain is known or perhaps knowable. Skepticism, freedom and independence of thought about matters of a more or less occult nature have their undoubted place and value in the outer ways of the world. But they are foreign to and inconsistent with the mental attitude appropriate to those who, on entering a hall of initiation, are supposed to tyle the door to the outside world and its conceptions, and, divesting themselves of all ideas there pre-acquired, to offer themselves as humble teachable pupils of a new and authoritative order of knowledge. Where everyone claims to be already possessed of a sufficiently satisfactory explanation of the universe and his place in it, or is content to get along without one, and in either case prefers his private judgment to any other that may be offered him, the soil for making initiates in any real sense is distinctly unfavorable. For such, however, these pages are not written. They are offered only to the minority of brethren eager to learn what Masonry has to teach them upon matters in which they earnestly seek knowledge and guidance.

Masonry, then, in exhibiting to them a simple ladder offers them a symbol the significance of which is calculated to open widely the eyes of their imagination. It is true that in the Instruction lecture the ladder is expressly referred to that of

Jacob in the familiar biblical episode, and that that ladder is
then given a moral significance and made to suggest the way
by which man may ascend from earth to heaven by climb-
ing its symbolic rungs, and especially by utilizing its three
chief ones representing the virtues Faith, Hope and Charity.
This moral interpretation is warranted and salutary. But it
is far from exhaustive, and conceals rather than reveals what
"Jacob's ladder" was really intended to convey to the perspicu-
ous when the compilers of our system gave it the prominence
they did. We may be assured they had a much deeper purpose
than merely reminding us of the Pauline triad of theological
virtues.

The ladder, then, covertly emphasizes the old cosmological teaching before referred to. It is a symbol of the universe and of its succession of step-like planes reaching from
the heights to the the depths. It is written elsewhere that the
Father's house has many mansions; many levels and resting
places for His creatures in their different conditions and degrees of progress. It is these levels, these planes and sub-planes,
that are denoted by the rungs and staves of the ladder. And of
these there are, for us in our present state of evolutionary un-
foldment, three principal ones; the physical plane, the plane
of desire and emotion, and the mental plane or that of the
abstract intelligence which links up to the still higher plane
of the spirit. These three levels of the world are reproduced
in man. The first corresponds with his material physique, his
sense-body; the second with his desire and emotional nature,
which is a mixed element resulting from the interaction of his
physical senses and his ultra-physical mind; the third with
his mentality, which is still farther removed from his physical
nature and forms the link between the latter and his spiritual
being.

The ladder, and its three principal staves, may be seen everywhere in nature. It appears in the septenary scale of musical
sound with its three dominants; in the prismatic scale of light

with its three primary colors; in our seven day scale of weekly time, in the septenary physiological changes of our bodily organism, and the similar periodicities known to physics and indeed to every branch of science. The perfect lodge has seven members, including three principal officers. The advancement of the third degree candidate to the East is by seven steps, the first three of which, it will be remembered, are given special significance.

Thus the universe and man himself are constructed ladder-wise, in an orderly, organized sequence of steps. The one universal substance composing the differentiated parts of the universe "descends" from a state of the utmost ethereality by successive steps of increasing densification until gross materialization is reached; and thence "ascends" through a similarly ordered gradation of planes to its original place, but enriched by the experience gained by its activities during the process.

It was this cosmic process which was the subject of the dream or vision of Jacob and which accounts for "Jacob's ladder" being given prominence in our symbolism. What was "dreamed" or beheld by him with super-sensory vision, is equally perceptible today by any one whose inner eyes have been opened. Every real initiate is one who has attained an expansion of consciousness and faculty enabling him to behold the ethereal worlds revealed to the Hebrew patriarch, as easily as the uninitiated man beholds the phenomenal world with his outer eyes. The initiate is able to "see the angels of God ascending and descending"—that is, he can directly behold the great stairway of the universe and watch the intricate but orderly mechanism of involution, differentiation, evolution, and re-synthesis, constituting the life-process. He can witness the descent of human essences or souls through planes of increasing density and decreasing vibratory rate, gathering around them as they come veils of matter from each, until finally this lowest level of complete materialization is reached, where the great struggle for supremacy between the inner and the outer man, between the spirit and the flesh, between the real self and the unreal selves and veils built round it, has to be fought out on the checker-work floor of our present existence, among the black and white opposites of good and evil, light and darkness, prosperity and adversity. And he can watch the upward return of those who conquer in the strife and, attaining their regeneration and casting off or transmuting the "worldly possessions" acquired during their descent, ascend to their Source, pure and unpolluted from the stains of this imperfect world. But to no man comes such vision as this unless he too be a Jacob who flees from the clash and hurly of secular activities into the solitude of his own soul, and in that barren wilderness interrogates himself and struggles agonizingly to penetrate the mystery of his existence, to read its purpose, and tear out the last secret of his own being. So, perchance, he may fall asleep, his head at last quietly pillowed upon that hard stone, against which hitherto he has been blindly dashing it. And then by the surrender of his own will and mental activities, and in the silence and quietude of the senses, his own inmost great Light may break, and from that newfound center he will see and know and find the answer to all his needs. For, in the words of an ancient record of initiation:

> the sleep of the body becomes the awaking of the soul, and the closing of the eyes true vision, and silence becomes impregnated with God. This happened to me when I received the supreme authentic Word. I became God-inspired. I arrived at Truth. Wherefore I give from my soul and whole strength, blessing to the Father.*

Jacob's vision and ladder, therefore, exemplify the attainment of initiation, the expansion of consciousness that comes when the Light of the center is found, and the cosmic vision that then becomes possible. The same truth is taught in a

---

*   Hermes, *Poemandres*, 1.30.

little treatise, of great instructiveness to every Mason, written by the initiate philosopher Porphyry in the third century and entitled *On the Cave of the Nymphs*. It is an exposition of a passage in Homer's *Odyssey*, which he shows likewise to be a veiled story of the soul's wanderings, of its crossing the rough seas of life and enduring the tempests and trials of this world, and finally perfecting itself and escaping into the haven of peace. The passage describes a certain dark cave, above which grew an olive-tree, and into which certain nymphs entered at one end and became busy in weaving purple garments for themselves; and it was not possible to leave the cave save by a gate at the other end and after having ceased to be satisfied with the pleasure of inhabiting that agreeable but benighted place and sought a way of escape. Porphyry thus explains the allegory: The dark cave is that of the body into which the soul (a "nymph" or spiritual being) enters and weaves around itself a garment of flesh and blood, and indulges in sense-gratification alien to its real nature. The nymph-soul has descended through the planes of the Cosmos until it has entered this cave by the "gate of man" (*i.e.*, by evolving to human status), and it can only leave it by passing out through the opposite gate, the "gate of the gods" (*i.e.*, by becoming perfected and divinized). This it cannot do save with the help of oil from the olive planted at the top of the cavern; the oil of wisdom which shall initiate the soul and guide it to the way out to the higher worlds and the regions of the blessed.

Porphyry's exposition continues thus:

> In this cave, therefore, says Homer, all external worldly possessions must be deposited. Here, naked and as a suppliant, afflicted, in body, casting aside everything superfluous, and renouncing all sensual energies, one must sit at the foot of the olive and consult with Minerva (Wisdom) by what means we may effectually destroy that hostile rout of passions which lurk insidiously in the secret recesses of

the soul.....It will not be a simple task to become liberated
from this sensible life; but he who dares to do this must
transmute himself, so that being at length divested of the
torn garments, by which his true self is concealed, he may
recover the ruined empire of his soul.[*]

The Mason who reads this parable will not fail to see
in it the allusion to the preparation of candidates for initiation, or to recognize that the cave and the olive-tree growing
above it correspond precisely with the grave of Hiram Abiff
and the sprig of acacia planted at its head. Both of these allude,
of course, to the human body in which the true spiritual self
of man lies buried and imprisoned, and from the bondage of
which it can only be freed by cultivating and lighting the oil
of wisdom (or, alternatively, of causing the sprig of acacia to
blossom) which will enlarge his consciousness and reveal to
him his path, through the universe.

We have each descended into this world by the steps of
Jacob's ladder; we have each to ascend from it by the same
steps. In some Masonic diagrams and tracing boards, upon the
ladder is exhibited a small cross in a tilted, unstable position
as if ascending it. That cross represents all who are engaged in
mounting the ladder to the heights, and who

. . . rise by stepping-stones
From their dead selves to higher things. [†]

Each carries his cross, his own cruciform body, as he ascends; the material vesture whose tendencies are ever at cross-
purposes with the desire of his spirit and militate against the
ascent. Thus weighted, each must climb, and climb alone; yet
reaching out—as the secret tradition teaches and the arms of

[*] On the Cave of the Nymphs, paragraph 16. Cited from the 1792 Thomas
     Taylor translation (reprinted by Phanes Press, 1991).—Ed.
[†] "In Memoriam A.H.H." (1859), chapter 1, lines 3-4.

the tilted cross signify—one hand to invisible helpers above, and the other to assist the ascent of feebler brethren below. For as the sides acid separate rungs of the ladder constitute a unity, so all life and all lives are fundamentally one, and none lives to himself alone.

Indeed life, and the ladder it climbs, are one and indissociable. The summit of both reaches to and disappears out of ken into the heavens; the base of both rests upon the earth; but these two terminals—that of spirit and that of matter—are but opposite poles of a single reality which cannot be known as a unity or otherwise than in its differentiated aspects of many planes, many mansions, many rounds or staves, except by him who has unified them in himself and become able to ascend and descend upon the ladder at will. But this is the privilege only of the initiate skilled in that science of life which teaches how to mount the *Scala Perfectionis*, as a famous classical work of the 15th century terms the ladder of initiation, known to Masons under the glyph of "Jacob's Ladder."

4. The Superstructure

The novitiate Mason is taught to regard his normal, natural personality as but a foundation-stone upon which he is recommended to erect a superstructure, perfect in all its parts and honorable to the builder. To how many does this instruction mean anything more than a general pious counsel to become merely a man of strong moral character and virtue? It is something, of course, to fulfill that elementary standard, which needs, however, no membership of a Secret Order for its accomplishment; but the recommendation implies a very different meaning from that, as a little reflection will show. It is not a recommendation merely to improve the condition of the already existing foundation-stone (the personality), but to erect upon that foundation something which which previously did not exist, something which will transcend and outrange it, although built upon it. For the reader who is unversed in

the deeper side of Masonic significance, and is unaware of the
hidden nature of it as thoroughly known to the original exponents of the science, the subject may prove difficult. It must
therefore be explained at the outset that the superstructure to
be erected is the organization of an ethereal or spiritual body
in which the skilled Mason can function in independence of
his physical body and natural personality.

The theory of Masonry presupposes that man is a fallen
creature; that his natural personality is a transient and unreal
expression of his true self as conceived in the divine mind; and
that, under appropriate tuition and self-discipline, he may become rebuilt and reorganized into the original condition from
which he has fallen. The present natural personality, however,
is the basis or foundation-stone out of which that reorgani-
zation can proceed, and within it already exists, though in a
condition of chaos and disorder, all the material requisite to
the purpose.

Building a superstructure upon one's present self involves
much more than merely improving one's moral character. It is
not a novice's task, although the advice to perform it is rightly
given in the Apprentice stage. It is a work of occult science, only
to be undertaken by those educated and skilled in that science.
It is the science to which the Christian Master referred in the
words: "Which of you, intending to build a tower, sitteth not
down first and counteth the cost, whether he have sufficient to
finish it? Lest, after he hath laid the foundation and is not able
to finish it, all that behold begin to mock, saying, 'This man
began to build but was not able to finish!'" (Luke 14:28-30)

Accordingly, the Mason desirous of building a tower or
superstructure should "sit down first and count the cost" by
acquiring a thorough understanding of what is involved; and
before he is able even to begin the erection of such a building, he will find a good deal of rough laborer's work has first to
be done upon himself in clearing the ground for the intended
structure.

There is an old Masonic degree, not comprised in our present Constitutions, devoted specially to this subject. It is called the degree of Grand Architect, and throws great light on the intention of those who, well understanding the secret science, made reference in our Ritual to the building of a superstructure.[*]

In that degree the reference is to "building structures in the air,"[†] and it is taught that this is the work only of grand architects, "being too great for inferior craftsmen, who only know by admiring them at a distance when done."

"Structures in the air!" All structures, save subterranean ones, rise into the air—the average reader will say; yet not buildings of brick or stone are here meant.

Again, building castles in the air is a familiar term for indulgence in day-dreaming and fanciful speculation; but, while all thought-energy is constructive and creates objective form upon the plane of mind, we may be assured that the sages who perpetuated Masonic science were innocent of recommending the practice of anything so futile and unpractical. The airy structure to which they allude is the formation of a super-physical ethereal body, a "body of mist" as Hesiod and other Greek classics describe it, in which the adept Mason may consciously function in the finer planes of life and apart from his

[*] The reference is to the degree of Grand Architecte from *Les Plus Secrets Mystères des Hauts Grades de la Maçonnerie Dévoilés ou le Vrai Rose-Croix* by M. de Bérage (1766). An English translation of the ritual is available, with critical notes by S. Brent Morris and Eric Serejski, in *Heredom: The Transactions of the Scottish Rite Research Society*, vol. 5, pp. 169–188.—Ed.

[†] In the original French this is *il faut nous occuper à en élever une troisième* ("we should be employed in the building of the third part of it") but Wilmshurst has read *en élevé* instead (i.e., "we should be employed with the third part of it on high"). Although the degree does not support Wilmshurst's notion of the "ethereal" building, it certainly alludes to the spiritual mastery needed to complete the Temple according to the divine plan. In this connection, the degree invokes Bezazel, the artisan who made the Ark of the Covenant in imitation of a heavenly design which kabbalistic tradition holds he was able to perceive through mystical wisdom. See Exodus 31:2–5, Zohar 2:152B & 2:234B—Ed.

gross physical organism, and in which he will continue to live when the latter has become permanently discarded. It is spoken of by Origen, the Christian father of the second century, as follows: "Another body, a spiritual and ethereal one, is promised us; a body not subject to physical touch, nor seen by physical eyes, nor burdened with weight, and which shall be metamorphosed according to the different regions in which it shall be. In that spiritual body the whole of it will be an eye, the whole of it an ear, the whole serve as hands, the whole as feet"*—implying that all the now distributed faculties will be unified in that body into one, as was the case with man before the fall and descent into matter and multiplicity.†

Let us justify these observations by some pertinent references to the subject in the great textbook of initiation science, the Volume of the Sacred Law; though they might be abundantly supplemented from other sources. Like the famous Orphic Hymns of the Pythagorean and Eleusinian mysteries, the Psalms of our Bible are an anthology of hymns of the Hebrew initiates and are full of Masonic allusion and instructiveness. In the 48th Psalm, the disciple of spiritual science is directed to take a walk around the symbolic city of Jerusalem; he was told to mark well its bulwarks, to observe its palaces, and particularly to pay attention to the great tower of the Temple, which, like a modern cathedral spire, rose into the air above all other buildings, so that he might not only himself appreciate the symbolism of what he saw, but might be in a position to interpret its significance to "them that come after"; that is, to junior students of the science.

He thus received a striking object-lesson in the analogy of material buildings to spiritual ones. In the massive defensive walls of the city he was to recognize the strength, perma-

---

*   Wilmshurst quotes Origen from F. Lamplugh's *The Gnôsis of the Light* (Watkins, 1918), p. 72. The original passage is found in St. Jerome's *Letter to Pammachius Against John of Jerusalem* § 26.—Ed.

†   For a fuller study of this subject, reference should be made to *The Subtle Body* by G. R. S. Mead (Watkins, 1919).

nence and resisting power of the spiritual organism or "holy city" which he must build for himself in exchange for, but upon the foundation of, the frail perishable temporal body. In the palaces of the mighty, with their gorgeous interiors and stores of costly furnishings and precious objects of art, he was to perceive that his own interior must become correspondingly beautified and enriched with spiritual treasures. But in the great heaven-pointing tower, to which his attention was specially directed, he was to see the symbol of a structure as far transcending his present temporal organism as the Temple-spire outranged the adjacent buildings at its feet. From this he was to deduce the necessity of building and projecting upwards from his lower organization, a "tower," a superior spiritual body, rising into and capable of functioning in the "air" or more tenuous and ethereal worlds than this physical one. This is the "structure in the air" which only "Grand Architects" are competent to raise; this is the "superstructure" which our Entered Apprentices are enjoined to aspire to building.

Let us turn next to the further pertinent information on the subject given by the apostle-initiate to his Corinthian pupils. He instructs them on this subject of superstructures. How is it possible to rear them? "How are the dead raised up, and with what body do they come?" (1 Corinthians 15:25) He is not speaking of the physically defunct, but of that condition of atrophied spiritual consciousness characterizing the normal animal man, which is always described as a state of "death" in the biblical and other writings on the subject. He proceeds to explain that the physical body itself cannot be raised, since corruption cannot inherit incorruption, but that nevertheless there can be a "resurrection from the dead" through a sublimation of its vital essences, which can be reorganized and reconstituted into a new body of subtle matter on a supra-physical level.

First comes the natural body we all wear to begin with; but out of it can be evolved a psychical body. The former is an entirely earthy vesture exhibiting an illusory unreal self to the world; the latter is the body of our true spiritual self (or "lord from heaven") which hitherto has remained masked and buried within that temporal vesture; "sown" in it as a seed, but capable of bursting its sheath and being raised from its former impotence to "power" (activity and conscious function). He properly speaks of it as one of the secrets and mysteries of initiation, and his familiar words may thus be paraphrased: "I am expounding to you a mystery, one of the arcana of initiation. We are not designed to remain always asleep in this drugged, deadened state of consciousness in which we are plunged, where we suffer the illusion that we are really alive, but are not. In the course of our evolution the due time comes for each of us to awake out of that sleep, and to become changed, transmuted; for our consciousness to be transposed to a higher level. We have borne the earthly human image; we have now to exchange it for an ethereal one of finer texture and purer quality. The change, the transposition of consciousness from the old to the new center, comes suddenly (though it may take long to prepare and purify ourselves for its coming). When it occurs it comes with an inwardly heard crash, like a trumpet-blast, as the nervous system and brain-structures react to the stress upon them involved in the transition."*

The apostle further explains that for this newly evolved ego or conscious center there is an appropriate body, for there are celestial as well as terrestrial bodies. There cannot be consciousness apart from a formal vehicle for it, and as the old earthy body has served (and will so continue to serve) for ordi-

---

* It must be explained that the "trumpet" and "last trumpet" are technical terms among initiates for the spiral, trumpet-shaped, whorls or vortices occurring in subtle matter under stresses, audible to those in whom the change occurs. The reference to the "sound of the last trumpet" stands for a physiological experience as the last fine physical strands of the old nature are, as it were, snapped and the nervous system re-electrified. In the East this experience is called the "end of the world," since for the initiate it means the termination of his old worldly consciousness and its replacement by one of a much more vivid and intense quality.

nary mundane purposes, so will the newly-evolved consciousness possess its own separate appropriate psychic or spiritual
body for function upon supra-physical levels. The initiate of
this high degree, therefore, will possess a twofold organization; his ordinary physical one (the "companion of his former
toils") and his supra-physical one, and will be able to utilize
and function in each. He will have built his "tower"; his "superstructure in the air."

The superstructure must be perfect in all its parts and so
be honorable to the builder. What are its parts?

Man, even in his natural, unregenerate, imperfectly
evolved state, is a highly composite creature. Blended with his
purely physical frame are three other supra-physical, but qua-
si-physical, bodies; his etheric body (the "double" or wraith),
his emotional or desire body, and his mental organization
or body; while over and beyond these, and not necessarily, in
functional alignment with them, exists his ultimate spiritual
self which distinguishes him from the sub-human creatures.
These are his "parts," and they are but too often extremely
ill-organized, uncoordinated and unbalanced. If they be imperfectly organized in the lower natural man, how can they
be expected to be able to contribute requisite sublimations of
themselves for the up-building of a body upon a higher level? All bodily and mental disease and infirmity originates in
disorder in these inner bodies, which disorder thereupon becomes reflected forwards and manifested in the physical husk.
Unless the inner natures be disciplined and organized before
the gross mortal vesture is shed at physical death, how can one
enter the ethereal kingdoms otherwise than "maimed," without a "wedding garment," and in a distorted shape, not perfect
in all its parts, and anything but honorable to the builder?

But, as we have long since seen, the first duty of every
spiritual craftsman is the purification and discipline of these
bodies, and the elimination from himself of all base metals
therein of which he has himself been an artificer. Only in pro-

portion to the achievement of this arduous task can he hope
to bring these "parts" into order, into subjection to his will,
and into coordinated function and alignment, and so in the
fullest sense stand erect, a just and upright man and Mason.
He need not trouble to know how his superstructure will develop or to what extent or measure of perfection he may have
built it. For it will become automatically built in his heights
proportionately as he schools himself in his depths and tests
his work by the continual application to it of the cross (which
is the square, level and plumb-rule in combination). When the
time comes for his consciousness to be raised to that superior
level and he hears the call "Friend, come up higher!" he will
find the superstructure he has been building in the darkness
below, perfect in all its parts and honorable to himself. He will
have climbed a section of the life-ladder; he will himself have
built, dedicated and consecrated King Solomon's Temple; and,
through the result of his own labor upon himself, that re-
splendent body will appear to him "more like the work of the
Great Architect of the universe than that of human hands."

There are, however, farther sections of the infinite ladder
to be climbed, even when this high level has been won. From
thence there remains still further building to be done, a body
to be fabricated manifesting still loftier wisdom, strength and
beauty. For was not the first symbolic Temple to be destroyed
and become replaced by a second, of which it is written that
"the glory of the former house is not to be compared with that
of the latter?" (Haggai 2:9)

But this still loftier work need not now be treated of. Let
it suffice if what has already been said assists any reader to the
building of his first superstructural Temple.

5. The Cable-Tow

These expositions are being offered in their present order with
a purpose. That purpose is to outline, as nearly and system-
atically as may be, the due sequence and progressive stages of

the work of spiritual craftsmanship or self-building. We have traced that work from its inception in the heart's desire to pass from darkness to light and attain a higher order of life and mode of being, through its stages of the outer and inward purification essential to that attainment, and through the crisis of a deeper gloom, a voluntary abnegation of and dying to all the attributes that go to constitute the natural personality, until the aspirant who endures all these to the end is finally rewarded by receiving his "crown of life," as the biblical metaphor very fittingly terms that exalted order of conscious being which marks the fulfillment of human spiritual evolution. And we have shown how, in winning that high degree of consciousness, he has simultaneously built for himself out of the sublimations of his original nature a new superstructural body appropriate to it and in which it can function. In the abounding wealth of the symbols and veiled verbal references in our rituals and instruction lectures to the details of this truly scientific work, there remain, however, many others needing explanation, some of which can now be considered more advantageously than at our earlier stage and with better chance of being understood.

One of these is the cable-tow. In my previous book it was explained that its use in the Entered Apprentice degree taught the beginner the useful lesson that he who has once felt within him the impulses of the central Light and been moved to seek it should never recede from his quest and, indeed, cannot do so without doing violence to the highest within him, a violence equivalent to moral suicide. At the same time, he is also enjoined not to be unduly precipitate, not ignorantly and rashly to rush forward in an unprepared inward state to grasp the secrets of his own being, in which case peril of another kind threatens him; but to proceed humbly, meekly, cautiously and under instructed guidance. The ancient maxim "Know thyself," was coupled with another—Ne quid nimis, "Nothing in excess"—for the science can only be learned and applied gradually. It will unfold itself more and more as it is diligently studied and pursued.

The foregoing explanation of the cable-tow is but a very partial one, and inculcates a salutary, but purely moral, piece of advice. The deeper significance is a psycho-physiological one, and has to do with the mysteries of the human organism. It should not be overlooked that the cable-tow is given prominence not only in the first degree. It is again mentioned in the obligation in the third degree, while it appears under another guise in that working-tool of the Master Mason which acts upon a center-pin. And finally it reappears in the Royal Arch degree as a cord or lifeline. It is requisite to understand what is involved in something to which such recurring prominence is given.

Let us first recall what has been already stated about the human organism being a composite structure of several natures or bodies (physical, etheric, emotional, and mental), fixated in a unity or synthesis; each of such bodies being constituted of gross or subtle matter, of differing density and vibratory rate, and the whole co-ordinated by the central divine Principle (which may or may not yet have come forward into the formal conscious mind, although there are few in whose awareness it is not lurkingly present and more or less active as "conscience.")

Thus the human constitution may be likened to a number of glass tumblers placed one within the other and with, say, a night-light (representing the central Principle) inserted in the inmost one. The glass of the tumblers may be imagined as of progressive thickness and coarseness, from within outwards, and some of them as colored, dirty, or not closely fitting in with the others. The coarser, dirtier, and more opaque the glasses, the less able will be the central light to shine through them; a single glass may be so opaque as to prevent the passage of the light through all the rest. Here, then, is an object lesson in the need for the inward purification of our various constituent sheaths, and for becoming "perfect in all our parts." As William Blake said very truly: "If the gates of human perception were thoroughly cleansed, we should perceive everything as it is—infinite; but man has closed himself up till he sees all things only through the narrow chinks of his own cavern."*

Another illustration. Human compositeness may be compared with the concentric skins or sheaths of a vegetable bulb (an onion, or hyacinth). Here the sheaths are all equally pure and co-ordinated; and because the bulb is perfect in all its parts or sheaths, and, when planted, fulfills the whole law of its nature, its life-force bursts its natural bonds, throws up a self-built superstructure into the air, and there effloresces into the bloom which is its "crown of life" or fullness of development. Man should do this, and, as we have shown, this is what the Mason is taught to do. But man having (what the bulb has not), freedom of will to fulfill or to violate the law of his nature, has chosen the latter course, and consequently by indulgence in perverse desire and wrongly directed thought, has fouled and disorganized his sheaths. Hence his spiritual darkness and his liability to all forms of disease. The central Principle cannot shine through his opacity, lighting up his mind and governing his desires and actions. It remains imprisoned within him., He sees, thinks and knows only from his self-darkened outer sheaths, and is misguided and illuded accordingly.

For a final example, let us turn to the instructive familiar episode in the Gospels of the storm overtaking a boat containing a number of men, of whom the Chief was "asleep in the hinder part of the boat." (Mark 4:38) The boat typifies the human organism; its occupants, its various parts and faculties, including the as yet unawakened master principle resident in its depths or "hinder part." An emotional upheaval occurs; the rough waves of passion threaten to wreck the whole party. A brain-storm arises; intemperate gusts of fright, wrongheaded-

* Paraphrased from Blake's *The Marriage of Heaven and Hell* (1790).—Ed.

ness, and mental uncontrol, make the position still worse. The extremity is sufficiently acute to awaken the master principle into activity whose beneficent power is able instantly to still those unruly winds, and waves, which suddenly are reduced to a great peace.

Every Master Mason, who is a real and not merely a titular one, is able to perform this "miracle" in himself; perhaps in others also. There is nothing super-natural about it to him. It is possible to him because he "has the Mason Word and second sight."* He both understands the composite structure of the human organism, can visually discern the disordered part or parts, and can apply healing, harmonizing, vibratory power from his own corresponding part to the seat of mischief, saying to this disordered mental part or that unruly emotional sheath, "Peace, be still!" (Mark 4:39) Every Master Mason is therefore also a master physician, able to benefit patients in a medical sense, and also to visualize the inner condition of those who look to him for instruction and initiation in a Masonic sense, to advise upon their interior needs and moral ailments, and help them to purify and align their disordered natures. But this is not possible save to one who himself has become pure and rectified in all his parts; the physician must first heal himself before he can communicate either physical or moral health to others.

This promise about the compositeness of the human structure and the existence in us of a series of independent, yet co-ordinated "parts" or sheaths, has been necessary before we can speak directly of the cable-tow. What is it that connects these parts? And are these parts dissociable from one another?

* This is a quotation from a poem entitled "The Muses' Threnodie" by Henry Adamson (1581–1637). The poem is notable for being the earliest evidence for an esoteric "mason-word" rather than just a password to identify guild members: "For what we do presage is not in grosse / For we be brethren of the rosie cross / We have the mason-word and second sight / Things for to come we can foretell aright..." (lines 909–912)—Ed.

We know that they are normally in close association and to this association applies the enjoinder that what God hath joined, man shall not put asunder. What the age-long process of evolution has built up with infinite patience and care is not to be tampered with for improper purposes, or even by well-meaning but, as yet, unenlightened experiment in the supposed interests of science; a point upon which the old Masters and teachers of our science are specially insistent, for reasons which now need not be entered upon.

Nevertheless, a measure of dissociation does occur naturally in even the most healthy and well-organized people (and of cases of abnormal psychic looseness of constitution we need not speak). It occurs in sleep, when the consciousness may be vividly active, whether in an orderly or disorderly manner; people "travel" in their sleep. It occurs at times of illness or violent shock. It may be induced by alcohol or drugs; the "anesthetic revelation" is a well recognized phenomenon. Under any of these conditions there may be a complete *ec-stasis*, or conscious standing out or away of the ego from the physical body.[†] Apparitions and even action at a distance are well accredited facts. Such phenomena are explicable only upon the suppositions of the existence of a subtler vehicle than the gross body, of the fact that consciousness becomes temporarily transferred from the latter to the former, and that the two are capable of conjoint function in complete independence of the physical brain and body.

What preserves the connection between the two "parts" thus disjointed, and makes possible their subsequent re-coalescence, is the "cable-tow." It is a connective thread of matter of extreme tenuousness and elasticity issuing from the physical abdominal region and maintaining the same kind of connection with the extended subtle body as the string with which a

† The word "ecstasy" is from the Greek word *ekstasis*, which means "standing away." The sense is similar to "being beside oneself," not in frustration but in religious awe or trance.—Ed.

boy flies a kite. As the boy can pull in the kite by the string, so does the extruded subtle body become drawn back to its physical base. Were the kite-string severed during the kite's flight, the kite would collapse or be blown away. Similarly, were the human "cable-tow" permanently severed, death would ensue and each of the severed parts go to its own place.

Biblically this human "cable-tow" is called the "silver cord" in the well known passage, "or ever the silver cord is loosed and the golden bowl is broken; then shall the body return to the earth and the spirit to God who gave it." (Ecclesiastes 12:6–7) "Silver" is the technical esoteric term for psychical substance, as gold is for spiritual, and iron or brass for physical. Its physiological correspondence is the umbilical cord connecting the child with its mother. Its analogue in ecclesiastical vestments is the girdle worn by the high priests of the Hebrews and by the priests and monastics of the Christian church.

Everyone unconsciously possesses the cable-tow, and it comes into use during sleep, when a less or greater measure of involuntary dissociation of our parts occurs. A Master, however, is one who has outgrown the incapacities to which the undeveloped average man is subject. Unlike the latter, he is in full knowledge and control of all his parts; whether his physical body be awake or wrapped in sleep, he maintains unbroken consciousness. He is able at will to shut off consciousness of temporal affairs and apply it to supra-physical ones. He can thus function at a distance from his physical body, whether upon the mundane or upon, higher planes of the cosmic ladder. His cable-tow, of infinite expansiveness, unwinds from his center-pin and, stretching like the kite-string, enables him to travel where he will in his subtle body and to rejoin and reanimate his physical one at will. Hence it is that the Master Mason is pledged to answer and obey all signs and summonses from any Master Mason's lodge if within the reach of his cable-tow; and such assemblies, it should be remembered, are contemplated therefore as taking place not at any physical location, but upon an ethereal plane. For corroboration of what is possible in this respect to a Master, one should reflect upon the instances of bi-location, passing through closed walls, and manifesting at a distance, recorded of the Great Exemplar in the Gospels. These are representative of what is feasible to anyone attaining mastership.

The cable-tow, therefore, is given prominence to the reflective craftsman as a help towards understanding his own constitution, and to foreshadow to him work that lies before him when is he fitted to undertake it—work which now may seem to him impossible and incredible. For as the Skirret (which is the cable-tow in another form)* is intended for the *skillful* architect to draw forth a line to mark out the ground for the intended structure, so the competent builder of the spiritual body will unwind his own "silver cord" when he learns how to function consciously on the ascending ladder of supraphysical planes, and to perceive the nature of the superstructure he himself is intended to construct.

Further importance attaches to the significance of the cable-tow from the fact testified to at the admission to our Order of every new candidate for ceremonial initiation. For all real initiation involves the use of the actual "silver cord" or lifeline; since such initiation always occurs when the physical body is in a state of trance or sleep, and when the temporarily liberated consciousness has been transferred to a higher level. Thence it subsequently is brought back to the physical organism, the cerebral and nerve centers of which become illumined, revitalized and raised to a higher pitch of faculty than was previously pos-

---

* American Masons are generally unfamiliar with the Skirret, which is one of the symbolic working tools of a Master Mason in the Emulation Rite worked commonly in England. Literally speaking, the skirret is a simple tool consisting of a center pin that is fixed in the ground and then used to measure the boundaries of a foundation before it is laid. The Emulation Rite provides a hint as to its Masonic meaning: "the Skirret points out that straight and undeviating line of conduct laid down for our pursuit in the Volume of the Sacred Law." See *The Complete Workings of Craft Freemasonry* (Lewis Masonic, 1982), p. 130.—Ed.

sible. The perspicacious Royal Arch Mason will not fail to perceive how this truth is dramatically exemplified in that degree.

This subject might be considerably extended, for while in a ceremonial system like the Masonic, only one initiation is portrayed (or, rather where initiation only occurs once), yet in the actual experience of soul-architecture, initiation succeeds initiation upon increasingly higher levels of the ladder as the individual becomes correspondingly ripe for them, able to bear their strain and to assimilate their revelations. What the Craft teaching and symbols inculcate is a principle common to every degree of real initiation that one may prove worthy to attain. For each upward step the candidate for the heights must be prepared as he is in the Entered Apprentice degree; at each there will be the same peril in turning back, and at each the same menace directed against rashly rushing forward.

6. The Apron

So much was said in my former volume, The Meaning of Masonry, in explanation of the Masonic apron, that it seems needless to speak at length of it again. Yet, to maintain continuity of thought, it seems desirable once more to refer to its symbolism at this point, since we have been closely considering the manner in which consciousness becomes expanded and enveloped in bodies or vehicles appropriate to that expansion; and we have been dealing with the arcanum or "mystery" propounded by St. Paul as to how the "dead" (the as-yet uninitiated and spiritually unquickened), are raised up to a new order of life and the new kind of embodiment they take on, or automatically fabricate, in the process.

Consciousness cannot exist without body. "To every seed (or conscious unit) its own body," says the apostle-initiate (1 Corinthians 15:38); or, as we Masons may paraphrase it, to every degree of life is allotted the appropriate apron, proclaiming the wearer's spiritual rank. As no one can enter the lodge unclothed with the apron, so no one can enter any of the unseen

worlds without wearing a body appropriate. There are bodies
terrestrial, adapted The to use on the lower planes of life; and
bodies apron celestial or ethereal, adapted to functioning on
higher ones. Man is a composite of many bodies, one within
the other; though ordinarily he is unaware of it and has not
yet organized them and come to know them separately, as the
initiate is expected to do.

The physical body is but one, and the grossest, of the terrestrial bodies; it is but a plaster of organized chemical particles, within and around which his subtler bodies exist, and
for which it forms a nexus or fixation point. When totally discarded at death it disintegrates; when partially abandoned in
sleep or anesthesia its energies persist passively, and connection with it is kept by the cable-tow or "silver cord." In each
case the ego, whether aware of it or not, stands minus its physical sheath and enclosed in its remaining ones. And a similar
divesting of each successive body may take place until only the
ultimate ego remains.

That ego, the ultimate divine principle in man, is represented by the triangular flap of the Masonic apron. The triangle (or pyramid form) is the geometrical symbol for Spirit
or Fire, and the ultimate Spirit of man may be likened to a
pointed flame or tongue of fire. (The word "pyramid" derives
from the Greek word pur, fire).

The body or form (or rather the succession of bodies or
forms), which that ego assumes on descending into manifestation through the ladder-like planes of the universe, aggregat-
ing to itself and organizing around itself material from each, is
represented by the lower quadrangular part of the apron. The
quadrangle, square or superfice is the geometrical symbol for
"body," "form," "physicalization." The quadrangle is further
appropriate because (1) all bodies are constituted of four elements, earth, water, air, fire; (2) because the human organism
is fourfold, a complex of four distinct departments, physical,
etheric, emotional and mental, and (3) because in man the

three sub-human kingdoms (mineral, vegetable and animal), are unified into the human synthesis.

The candidate's first investiture with the apron is symbolic therefore of his ego's entrance into this world, and becoming clothed with form or body. He is meant to realize himself as a sevenfold being, perfectly constituted originally in the Divine Mind; his triangle of Spirit combining with the quadrangle of materialized form to make up the perfect number seven. He is meant to realize that he has descended to a condition of embodiment and limitation of consciousness for the purpose of acquiring experience in those conditions, and of performing certain work upon himself which shall raise him to full realization of his own ultimate nature and of the divine purpose in him, and that though his present state or form is one of restriction and humiliation, it will never disgrace him if he never disgraces it.

In the first degree, the triangular flap of the apron is kept erect. In the second it is lowered. Thereby is denoted the physiological truth that the ego or human spirit on entering this world at birth does not immediately attain full embodiment, but at first is, as it were, an over-hovering presence, organically connected with the body, but only gradually taking possession of it. We recognize this apron truth in practical life. Moral and legal responsibility is never attributed to a child under seven years of age, for the moral sense has not yet developed. Important physiological changes connected with puberty occur at the age of fourteen. Civic responsibility is denied until twenty-one is reached. The basic reason for all this is the occult truth that the ego does not attain its maximum of incarnation until twenty-one. Accordingly it is not until age is reached that a man is presumed competent to enter the Craft and undertake the science of himself.

As the ego immerses itself in its body and works upon it, it creates changes in it, whether for good or evil. It either organizes or disorganizes its vehicles according to its will and desires.

It becomes an artificer in metals, whether base or precious; it either stores itself with ornaments and jewels and the invaluable furniture of self-knowledge, or with useless trumperies and grotesque contrivances of which sooner or later it must get rid. Assuming its activities to have been wisely directed, they are evidenced in the apron by the blue rosettes* imposed upon it in the second degree; if they are persisted in and the spirit more and more subjugates and controls the form, that increasing domination and the further progress made in the science are testified to by the additional elaborations found in the apron in the third degree. Still more advanced progress is evidenced by further changes and beautification of the apron in the Royal Arch degrees, and in the Grand Lodges of provinces, and of the nation.

The Tau displayed upon the apron worn by those of Master rank is a form of the Cross, and also of the Hammer of Thor, of Scandinavian religion. It is displayed triply, to signify that the wearer has brought his three lower natures (physical, emotional, and mental) under complete control; that he has crucified them and keeps them repressed by the hammer of a strong will.

The further important point should be noticed that the apron covers the creative, generative organ of the body; and it is especially to these that the significance of the Tau attaches. Spiritual self building and the erection of the "superstructure" are dependent upon the supply of creative energy available from the generative nervous center, the "powerhouse" of the human organism. Thence that energy passes upwards through other ganglionic "transformers" and, reaching the brain, becomes finally sublimated and transformed to consciousness.

* American Masons may be unfamiliar with the rosettes, which originated in Europe well after Masonry became established in the new world. They are ribbons in the form of round badges affixed to Masonic aprons in some jurisdictions. None exist on the Apprentice apron, two on the Fellow Craft, and three on the Master Mason's apron.—Ed.

Conservation of that energy is therefore indispensable both for generating consciousness and providing the material for the finer vehicle or "superstructure" in which that consciousness may function; the life-energy is always creative, either in the direction of physical propagation or in that of super-physical up-building; hence the importance attached in religious spheres to celibacy.

It should also be noted that in the three Craft degrees, the investiture with the apron is made in the West; and not by the Master, but by his principal officer who is deputed to bestow it. The meaning behind this important detail is that while the human ego is resident in this temporal world ("the West"), Nature, as the chief officer and deputy of Providence, supplies it with bodies of her own material and temporal substance. But in all cases beyond those three, the investiture takes place in the "East"—the realm of spirit, and from the hands of the Master himself. For the progressed soul receives a clothing beyond Nature's power to supply; and, without intermediate hands, "God giveth it a body as it pleaseth Him," and to every such soul its own body, according to its measure of progress and consciousness.

7. The Wind

The instruction lectures of the first degree (unfortunately not used in some lodges), contain a curious reference to the blowing of the wind, which must puzzle a good many minds. *

---

*   This feature is unknown in American Masonry, but evident in the British Emulation workings that Wilmshurst knew:

    Q How blows the wind in Masonry?

    A Favourably, due East or West.

    Q Why so.

    A To cool and refresh men at labour.

    Q It has a further allusion?

    A To that miraculous wind which proved so essential in working the happy deliverance of the children of Israel from their Egyptian bondage. [*The Complete Workings of Craft Freemasonry* (Lewis Masonic, 1982), pp. 209–210.]

What has the wind to do with Masonic work, and why should it be particularly favorable to that work when blowing from East to West or vice versa?

Again we must look below the letter of the reference. The subject has not been introduced without purpose and instructiveness, to discern which will once more reveal the wisdom of the compilers and the crypticism with which they purposely shielded it when preparing our system for more or less common use.

The wind referred to is not the atmospheric breeze. It is that Wind (Gr. *pneuma*) which "bloweth where it listeth" (John 3:8); the wind of the spirit; the currents of divine energy.

The "East" and the "West" are not our ordinary geographical directions of space. In initiatic and Biblical language, as in the quarters of the lodge, the East is the realm of spirit and light; the West that of matter and darkness, the place of the disappearing sun. Man partakes of both; he is polarized east-to-west, as Spirit-Matter in one.

When, mystically, the wind blows east-to-west, a current of divine energy has set in towards the west, stimulating, vitalizing and enlightening it. When it blows west-to-east, man has himself directed a current of aspiration from his own spirit eastwards to God. The wind is therefore said to be specially favorable to Masonic work when blowing from either of those points of the mystical compass. When the Mason sends up his aspirations to the heights, as he should perpetually be doing, he is as a dynamo generating and transmitting an electric current upwards; that is, eastwards. When the divine fire

A still older version from William Preston's version says:

Q   How blows the wind?

A   Favourably it would waft him to a home, be it east, be it west.

Q   For what purpose should it so blow?

A   That he may have rest and refresh himself under the rays of the meridian sun, should he bear this testimony of claim to our favour. [P. R. James, The First Lecture of Free Masonry by William Preston, *Ars Quatuor Coronatorum*, vol. 82 (1969), p. 148.] —Ed.

descends upon himself, a similar current has set in westwards. It is written elsewhere and in the same sense, "As the lightning shineth from the east unto the west, so is the coming of the Son of Man" (Matthew 24:7) into the personal consciousness.

Prayer, upward aspiration in the above sense, is a practical scientific necessity for the work of the spiritual craftsman. He himself is but as the leaden weight swinging at the lower end of the string of the plumb-rule. The string itself is as the connecting wire between that weight and the top of the plumbrule, a wire through which a current may pass up or down. Until that instrument is held erect, and the leaden weight brought to stillness and steadiness, it is ineffective for any form of work. So long as man is spiritually unaligned and out of plumb with his spiritual pole, directness of current between them is impossible. When that current is established the lead of darkness and ignorance may become transmuted into the gold of conscious light and wisdom by the alchemy of the Spirit.

Real initiates have always known there to be both special times and seasons, and special localities favorable to inducing the flow of currents of divine energy; but of these the modern Mason has not yet come to learn, though there are references to them in his system. The two solstices and equinoxes are such times, and others are known in the greater churches whose calendar of feasts and fasts have been based upon this principle. The festivals of the two Masonic patron saints, St. John Baptist at midsummer, and St. John the Divine at midwinter, have special bearing upon favorable times for spiritual craftsmanship, but the former is now ignored, and the latter profaned. The matter may be left to the reflection of brethren. When the Craft comes better to realize its purpose and science, these times and seasons will be taken advantage of for the furtherance of both individual and collective Masonic work.

The teaching in the instruction lecture upon the wind is supplemented by a reference to the escape of the Israelites from Egyptian bondage under their master Moses, who caused a mighty east wind to blow, dividing the waters of the Red Sea to permit of their safe passage, which waters then rolled back and overwhelmed Pharaoh and his pursuing army.

Again, the bearing of this episode is lost upon the average brother, who for want of a key fails to see its relevance to any form of Masonry. And, indeed, it carries us into much deeper water than the average mind bathes in, although to those versed in initiation science, the striking biblical incident masks and prefigures an equally momentous one in the individual life of everyone who seeks to fulfill his own spiritual evolution.

The allusion is to the important crisis which occurs when the personal soul of the aspirant ardently aspires for complete liberation from the tyranny of the flesh. It is then possible, in proper cases—and this was part of the office of the old mysteries—for one who is a real master so to act upon and separate his disciple's interior organic structures as to effect a permanent liberation of the latter's consciousness from sensual bondage. The "waters" that are then "divided" are what have previously been explained as those of the fluidic subtle body of desire and emotion, which normally constitute an untraversable barrier between the highest and the lowest elements in our nature. "Wretched man that I am, who shall deliver me from this body of death?" (Romans 7:24) exclaimed one who afterwards attained delivery. For the "body of death" is made up of all those lower natures in us which inhibit consciousness in the spirit; and, as we have elsewhere stated, it is dissociable by a competent adept-master, who holds the keys of life and death (i.e., consciousness and unconsciousness in the spirit). The higher nature of the disciple is then liberated from the bondage of the lower; his waters are divided; he passes through them into permanent safety from the Pharaoh-like tyranny of his material vesture; the still pursuing tendencies of which are checked, overwhelmed and shut off when the temporarily held up waters are permitted to roll back to their former channel, to the extreme joy of the now liberated disciple.

This is an incident of real initiation, and it is achievable only under the guidance of the equivalent of a Moses, a real Master. To those unversed in the deeper aspects of initiation science, what cannot here be more than briefly explained may appear incredible, as would much more that lies concealed beneath the symbols and the text of the Masonic system. But those responsible for compiling or inspiring that system were clearly deeply versed in much that they permitted themselves to do no more than hint at, and it remains for reflective Masons to penetrate their disguises by their own research, intuition and perspicacity.

8. Seeking a Master

The junior brother learns that, as a Mason, his duty is to seek a Master and from him gain instruction, and usually supposes that by making acquaintance with the Worshipful Master of his lodge, and learning by rote the rituals and lectures, he is fulfilling that duty. If he desires nothing more than ceremonial Masonry, he is doubtless doing all that need be expected of him. But if he be in earnest quest of that to which ceremonial Masonry is but an entrance-portal, he may be interested in the following considerations.

It is axiomatic in the traditional secret wisdom that real initiation is not to be looked for save at the hands of one who has himself experienced it. And it is equally axiomatic that "when the disciple is ready, the Master will be found waiting." The modern Masonic student will be well advised to accept both these axioms as being as valid today as they have ever been in the past.

A Master is not easily found. But neither is he often properly sought. "Ask, seek, knock," are simple words to say with the tongue. Their putting into effective operation is a task involving persistent and concentrated will. Under no circumstances does a Master ever proclaim himself as such; he must be sought, must be clearly recognized and wholeheartedly accepted as one; and you may have grave doubts of his status and your own judgment about him before according him that confidence. You might live in close contact with a Master for years without suspecting the fact. Recognition being due to spiritual rapport, to vibratory harmony and to intuitional certainty; until you possess these a Master's physical personality will convey no more to you than any other man's. But of one thing be assured; the Master will know *you* through and through long before you recognize *him*, or perhaps even realize that you are seeking him.

Exoterically, in the operative mason's trade, the youth proposing to enter a building guild had first to find a master mason who would accept him as his apprentice and to whom he became bound for seven years, the master making himself responsible for his maintenance and training. In spiritual craftsmanship precisely the same method applies. The master has first to be sought and found, and, if the disciple be accepted, he must be served and implicitly obeyed for a similar probationary period, the master assuming a real (not a nominal) spiritual sponsorship for the pupil. The association not being for any temporal advantage but for purely selfless spiritual advancement, the intimacy is of the closest, as the responsibility is of the gravest, character. For the apprentice is to become spiritually integrated with the Master. To use the beautiful touching simile of the greatest of Masters, as a hen gathers her chickens under her wing (*cf.* Luke 13:34), so is the pupil to become gathered and built into the very being of his teacher. The real initiation (or rather sequence of initiations) the pupil hopes in due course to attain cannot be achieved until this intimate relationship exists.

In the days of the ancient mysteries, masters were to be found resident in the seclusion of the temples, for initiation science was then an organized institution, publicly recognized.

In the Orient, no such formal organization has obtained, but the practice, both in the past and today, is for the aspirant to seek and find his appropriate master, the onus of searching being upon the former, and serving as a test of his earnestness and perspicuity. The Master is there termed a guru (defined as "one who removes the veil of darkness from the spiritual eyes of the pupil"), and the accepted pupil a chela or spiritual child, in the same sense that St. John addresses his pupils as "little children." (1 John 2:1) The ancient Sanskrit word guru passed from India to Asia Minor and Greece, and reappears in the latter part of the name of such ancient initiates as Protagoras, Anaxagoras, Pythagoras. The last-mentioned of these literally means the *pitta* (or *pater*) *guru*, the master or father-teacher, as in fact he was in his day; and the continuity of both the science and of the title *guru* is further evidenced by the fact that that title is preserved both in Hebrew and in Masonry in the name of Hiram Abiff (spelled also in the Scriptures as Huram and Churam Abiff). Hiram Abiff has precisely the same meaning as Pythagoras, the father-teacher, or alternatively the "teacher from the father." The Egyptian form of the name Hiram is Hermes, the teacher of the secret or "hermetic" science and wisdom, and the student is strongly urged to study those two important ancient treatises of initiation science, the *Divine Poemander of Hermes* and *The Shepherd of Hermas.* *

A Master, while rejoiced to find a suitable pupil, does not accept him without subjecting him to severe preliminary tests. He "knows what is in man." (John 2:25) No hypocrisy deceives him. He discerns the thoughts and desires of the heart of the intending candidate, and sees whether the latter is properly prepared there, and really anxious and ready for the work involved. Of this, an example came to my knowledge, which it

* "Shepherd" is the ancient and biblical word signifying "Initiator" or "Hierophant." Hence "the Good Shepherd," "the Great Shepherd of the sheep," "The Lord is my Shepherd." The "Shepherds watching their flocks" at the time of the Nativity were not rustics or farmers, but spiritual adepts in charge of groups of initiate pupils.

may be useful to record, and to remember in connection with the acceptance of Masonic candidates. It was as follows.

A young man in India sought out a venerable master there and asked to be accepted as a pupil and trained for initiation; he professed to want to find the Light, to know God at first hand. The old sage, after a searching glance into the aspirant's inward condition, discerned that the latter, while not insincere, was still a long way from readiness, and far from being sufficiently detached in desire for worldly possessions and sensual enjoyments; and, explaining this, he firmly but kindly sent him away to exhaust or merge himself of these attractions, but with the suggestion that he might present himself again in two years' time. After two years, the young man returned, found the old master bathing in the river at the foot of his garden, and from the riverbank renewed his application. Again the old man read his visitor's heart to its depths and perceived how divided it still was between the claims of the outer and the inner life; but, calling him down into the river, he laid his hand upon the young one's head and gently pressed and held it below the surface of the water. Presently the young man forced it above the surface. "Why did you do that?" he was asked. "I was obliged to do so to find breath." Then came the master's answer: "When you want God and the inward light as badly as you just now wanted breath, you may come back to me and you shall have your desire. But for the present you want other things as much, and you can't have both." Like the other young man in the gospels, the applicant went away sorrowful; but he had found his eventual master and gained from him the instruction suitable to him at the moment.

How, where, is one to seek one's master, if he be so secluded, so hard to find? He may be sought both without and within oneself. He should first be sought in every event of the daily life, in the person of everyone you meet. Finding him depends on the intensity of your search. "Seek and ye *shall* find" is not a vain promise. Look not to meet immediately with some learned or impressive personality capable of giving you all truth in tabloid form in a few hours. Final truth cannot be communicated at all from one person to another orally; it exists already within yourself and needs only to be dug out and liberated. Socrates—himself a Master, though the son of a poor midwife—used to joke that he had inherited something of his mother's profession in that his task was to help others to bring truth to birth out of themselves; and in the same sense the medieval teachers speak of using "the obstetric hand" in eliciting truth from their pupils rather than of instilling it into them. For the pupil has first to learn to clear away his own falsities and unrealities, so that what is already central in himself may no longer be obscured, but shine out, in its own self-conscious light.

When the time is ripe and the pupil in a deep sense ready, he may come to meet a master literally and in personal wise. But a master, being one who has evolved in his spirit, is no longer to be thought of as a separate independent person, although displaying a separate personality and presence to the world. He is integrated with others of the same rank; he is part of a group, all the members of which are conscious on the plane of spirit. And spirit is universal, not fettered by place, time, or space. What the group perceives, each of its parts sees, and vice versa. Remember the All-seeing Eye, the universal Watchman, that perceives *you* and knows the quality of your spirit, though you yourself know nothing of it.

Until, then, a master is met with personally, the search should persist in confidence that he will be found. Responses, justifying your confidence and demonstrating that the Eye is watching you, will come in unsuspected ways to the earnest seeker; perhaps from a chance passage in an apparently quite irrelevant book you may be led to pick up; perhaps from a casual meeting with a stranger, an offhand remark, the conversation of a friend who speaks more wisely and pointedly to you than he himself realizes. Through such and other ways may the veiled master look or speak to you, and proportionately to the ardor of your search will you find evidences of his presence and watchfulness. A saintly woman, a great British poetess, so keenly sought a Master in the details of daily life that she would pick up torn scraps of paper in the street on the chance that they might reveal his name or yield some evidence of him. Another seeker traveled across the world in blind faith that somewhere the unknown Master would be found. One day in the street of a foreign city the recognition came suddenly; before a stranger in the crowd the seeker stopped, saying "Master, teach me!"—and the search was ended.

"The Master" to be sought, then, is a comprehensive term—abstract and mystical if you will, but standing for a reality embracing many personal masters integrated in it. In seeking a personal master, one seeks also the group of which he is a member; in seeking the impersonal master one may be brought into personal contact with one of that group. Life in the realm of Spirit is a unity, not a diversity, and for Masonic seekers the wide world over, of whatever nation or creed, there is but one Grand Master and Hierophant, but He can manifest and deputize through diverse channels. As in the Craft lodge there is but one Master, yet many of equal rank capable of representing him and doing his work, so has the world's Grand Master in the heights His associates and deputies here in its dark depths.

So far we have spoken only of seeking exteriorly, for an outward personal master. But the search can and should also be made interiorly, within oneself; for what is sought subjectively and spiritually can then more readily come to be realized and found objectively. The great Indian manual of initiation (the Bhagavad Gita) therefore teaches:

There lives a Master in the hearts of men
Who makes their deeds, by subtle-pulling strings.
Dance to what time He will. With all thy soul
Trust Him, and take Him for thy succour.

So shalt thou gain,
By grace of Him, the uttermost repose,
The Eternal Peace. *

Seek therefore to realize the master in the heart. Conceive him imaginatively. Build up in your constant thought a mental image of him, invested with the nature and qualities of that master-soul to whom you look to raise you from your present deadness, to remove the stone from your sepulcher, and to utter to your inmost self that vibrant word of liberating power, "Lazarus, come forth!" For until you have in yourself something in common with him, points of fellowship with him—be it but a bare desire for resemblance—how shall you expect to be raised into fullness of identic relationship with him, to be "gathered as a chicken under his wing?"

Our science in its universality limits our conception of the master to no one exemplar. Take, it says, the nearest and most familiar to you, the one under whose aegis you were racially born and who therefore may serve you best; for each is able to bring you to the center, though each may have his separate method.

To the Jewish brother it says, take the Father of the faithful, and realize what being gathered to his bosom means. To the Christian brother, it points to Him upon whose breast lay the beloved disciple, and urges him to reflect upon what that implies. To the Hindu brother it points to Krishna, who came and rode in the same chariot with Arjuna, and bids him look to a similar intimate union. To the Buddhist it points to the Maitreya of universal compassion, and bids him reflect upon him till he become drawn beneath his Bô-tree; and to the Muslim it points to his Prophet, and the significance of being clothed with the latter's mantle.

Let the earnest craftsman, then, seek a master where and how he will. He cannot—*experto crede*—fail to find. Failure

---

* Bhagavad Gita 18.61–62. Paraphrased by Wilmshurst from Sir Edwin Arnold's famous translation, *The Song Celestial.*—Ed.

to find will be due to his having failed, rightly, and from his heart, to seek.

9. Wages

Initiates of the secret science in the past ("our ancient brethren") are said to have been paid wages. The wages, we are told, were paid in the porchway of the Temple; and, much or little, they were accepted without demur, because of the recipients' complete confidence in their employers and the recognition that only so much would be received as their work was actually worth. The Masonic tradition asserts that the wages were not paid in cash—cash was of no use to those who had already learned to do without money and metals—but in corn, wine, and oil. (Note the threefold form of the wages).

Wages of the same kind are still paid to real craftsmen in the same place, and in the same mode. The porchway of the Temple figures the outer natural life which forms a portal to an inner supernatural life at the central sanctuary which we have not yet consciously reached, but to which we labor to ascend by an in-winding stairway, gradually rebuilding body and mind on the way with a view to acquiring a new reconstituted organism appropriate and adapted to that sublime degree of life.

Such a new body and mind require sustenance to build them, and the food we consume becomes built into our organism. What we eat, we become. Corn goes to body-building, the fashioning of substantiality and structural form. Wine goes to the vitalizing and stimulating of the mind, strengthening the intellect, deepening the inner vision. Oil is a lubricant for the system, enabling its parts to run smoothly and without friction.

In their higher symbolism corn (or bread) and wine relate to those of the altar, and were eucharistic elements in the mysteries long before the Christian Master in a certain "upper room" (or higher level of application) took over and gave a new application to the wheat of Ceres and the wine of Bacchus-Dionysos; while oil, the crushed out and refined product of the olive, refers to that wisdom which is the ultimate essence of experience and knowledge, and which has been associated, in the different mystery teachings, with Minerva, with Solomon, and with the Mount of Olives.

The spiritual craftsman not only earns his own wages proportionately to his work; his own labors automatically supply them. God, as his employer, has already lodged them within him in advance; he has only to appropriate them as he becomes justly entitled to them by his own labors, as the sons of Jacob found their money restored to them in their corn-sacks.

The Mason is himself likened to an ear of corn, nourished by a fall of the water of life.* In virtue of the animal element in his nature he is himself "the ox that treadeth out the corn," (Deuteronomy 2:4) separating his own golden grain from the stalk that bore it. He is himself the "threshing floor of Araunah," † winnowing his own chaff from his own wheat. He treads his own wine-press alone; in singleness of effort and in the solitude of his own thought distilling his own vintage, until the cup of his mind runs over with the wine of a new order of intelligence. He is his own oil-press, and out of his own experience and self-realization extracts wisdom—that oil which anoints him with a joy and an ability above his fellows, and that runs down to the "skirts of his clothing,"‡ manifesting itself in his personality and in all his activities.

---

*   Wilmshurst refers to an old practice, not currently followed by many jurisdictions in the United States, where the Masonic candidate in each degree is told to understand the password as a new "name" of sorts.—Ed.

†   A piece of land purchased by King David, which later became the site of the Temple of Solomon and the Second Temple (cf. 2 Samuel 24:15–25). Thus it is a symbolic conjunction of the functions of the Temple and of the threshing floor to which Wilmshurst alludes.—Ed.

‡   An allusion to Psalm 133, which is recited during the circumambulation of the Entered Apprentice degree.—Ed.

Corn, wine, and oil, are therefore laid upon the altar at the consecration of every Masonic lodge; they are the emblems of a craftsman's wages. Upon the collars of Grand Lodge Officers are displayed ears of wheat and sprays of olive, the symbolic indication that those who arrive at the summit of their profession possess that which they exhibit, and are able to minister bread and wine and oil to those below them in the Order.

There are less agreeable forms of wages, however, but such as also are to be received without scruple or mistrust, for they are both disciplinary and signs of progress. A man cannot set up to re-form his old nature and readjust his interior constitution without feeling it, or without unsettling the fabric of his emotional and mental sheaths. Accordingly, it is a common experience with those who take themselves seriously in hand in the task of self rebuilding that unexpected obstacles suddenly arise; the wages that come to them are those of adversity in temporal affairs, sickness, the turning away of former friends, and the like. There is good reason for this. Within ourselves are sown the seeds of all our past activities and emotional tendencies, good or evil. Within ourselves are stored all our old mind-forms and fabrications of base metal. To try to disturb the former or to divest ourselves of the latter, promotes immediate reaction from them.

He who deliberately invokes the Light upon himself, as the earnest Masonic aspirant does, *ipso facto* utters, with corresponding intensity, a challenge to his own bad past, his own unreal self. And if his invocation be effective, the Light streaming into him from his own dormer-window, while giving him illumination, will also play upon and stimulate in him all that is undesirable, as sunlight stirs to activity the unpleasant insects dwelling in darkness beneath a stone that is suddenly removed from an old position. Light impartially affects both the good and evil in oneself, as the sunshine causes a rose to bloom, and a lump of carrion by its side to putrefy. It induces new growth in a spiritual sense, but it also, and at the same time, accelerates the germination of seeds implanted in us, which, but for it, would continue to lie dormant and unmatured until a more favorable time.

Under the discipline of initiation the seeds or compressed results of one's own past, the potential reactions from one's own former actions and inaction, all that goes to make up a man's fate and that, if unchecked, will shape his future destiny, are brought to a sudden head and crisis; the normal slower development they would have undergone, if not so interfered with, becomes interrupted, expedited. It is often as though vials of undeserved wrath break upon the devoted head of him who at last has struck the road to salvation, and is resolved at all costs to follow it. And yet these are the wages he receives for his laudable enterprise!

Lacking self-knowledge as yet, ignorant of what is latent in him, not realizing that the path of initiation is one of intensive culture and accelerated evolution, he may become dismayed from further pursuing his quest, unless he be made aware that these wages are actually due to him, that they represent his past earnings, that he is justly entitled to them, and that the sooner the debit and credit sides of his own self-written judgment-ledger are balanced, the freer will he be to proceed with his newly undertaken building-work.

"The wages of sin are death" (Romans 6:23)—death in the sense of being spiritually unconscious, however vigorously alive in other ways. "Sin" in all or any of its forms is, in its final analysis, disharmony induced by the assertion of the unreal personal self in disalignment with the impersonal universal self, the holy spirit. But the path of initiation involves the obliteration of all sense of the personal self. The just and perfect man and Mason is therefore one who is utterly selfless; being selfless he is sinless; and being sinless he stands in, consciously shares, and becomes the instrument of, the divine kingdom, power and glory.

10. The Law of the Mount

In Masonry, as in the Scriptures and every other ancient expression of mystical teaching, there is frequent allusion to mountains and bills, and to the work of lodges and Chapters being, conducted upon them.

Let it be understood at once that in no case is the allusion to any physical mountain or geographical position, but to the spiritual elevation of the work undertaken by some particular group or school of initiates. Spiritual science has nothing to do with material things or places, save in so far as the latter serve as a foundation-stone or point of departure for achieving spiritual results.

From time immemorial the Vedists of India have spoken of their sacred Mount Meru, which, later in history, becomes reproduced among the Hebrews as Mount Moriah. The Greeks had their Mount Olympus and Parnassus, on the summits of which dwelt the Gods. The Israelites obtained their law from divine hands on Mount Sinai; the Christians theirs from the Mount of Olives. The woodwork for Solomon's Temple came from the mountains of Lebanon. The gospels tell of the "exceeding high mountain" of temptation (Matthew 4:8) and of the mount of transfiguration (cf. Mark 9:2–10). Prometheus was immolated upon a mountain of the Caucasus (or Ko-Kajon, i.e., "ethereal space"), and Christ upon the hill of Calvary. Medieval Christian mystical tradition tells of the hidden sanctuary of the mysteries and the holy Grail built upon Mont Salvatch (the mount of safety or salvation) in the Pyrenees (which is another form of "Parnassus.")

None of these mountains are situated in this world, in time or place. The names are mystical names associated with super-physical heights to which man in his spiritual consciousness may ascend. Mountains bearing those names, or some of them, do exist on the map, but their names and the ideas they connote existed long before they were given a local association for symbolic purposes. There is scarcely a country without its sacred mountain that reminds its inhabitants of the heavenly heights and to which sacred traditions are not attached. The snow-clad Himalayas have always typified the eternal heavens to the East; Fujiyama is the sacred mountain of Japan, as Snowdon is of Britain; and if such places have been, as indeed they have, the scenes of religious practices, their sanctity derives less from what has occurred there than from the ideas that resulted in those practices. The names of these sacred mountains are drawn almost always from ideas representative of the religion of the district, and constitute a sort of spiritual geography which nations of great spiritual genius, such as the Indians, the Greeks, and the Hebrews, have been faithful in preserving. Subsequently the materializing tendencies of the human mind literalize and localize what originally existed as a purely spiritual idea.

When initiates of the past are said to have held lodges and performed their work upon this or that hill or mountain, the meaning is that they were engaged in work of a high spiritual order and efficacy—work entirely beyond the conception of the average modern and merely ceremonial Mason. The actual place at which they met for such work may or may not have been upon a physical eminence. Often it was not, as abundant evidence might be brought to show. The entirely super-physical nature of their work may be deduced from an old Scottish degree of advanced Masonry, which speaks, with a dry humor that to the inexpert eye will seem grotesque and irreverent, of their lodge having originally been held upon a hill in the North of Scotland, a place "where a cock never crowed, a lion never roared, and a woman never tattled." Now in traditional esoteric terminology, as also in the Bible, the "North" signifies that which is spiritual and ever unmanifested, as the other three cardinal points of space indicate varying degrees of spiritual manifestation. The allusion to cock-crow is to the guilty conscience of Peter, which could only exist in the world of time and in one who is spiritually imperfect. The allusion to the lion is to the Evil One "going about as a roaring lion" (1 Peter 5:8) in the lower world, but unable to enter the Paradisal world; while the third reference is to the contemplative silence of the soul (the "woman") upon that high plane of life of which the Psalmist says that "there is neither speech nor language but their voices are heard among them." (Psalms 19:4) In the *Odyssey*, Homer testifies to the same truth when Ulysses is told in regard to certain mysteries, "Be silent; repress your intellect, and do not speak; such is the method of the Gods upon Olympus."

It must be left to the reader's own research and reflection to deduce the nature of the spiritual work undertaken by real initiates; he will discover that it is work that is not performed in the physical body or with that body's faculties, but upon the ethereal planes and with a higher order of faculty than the average man of today has learned to cultivate. For a striking instance of the kind of work implied, reference can be made to the narrative contained in the 19th and 24th chapters of Exodus, describing a lodge of the elders or adept-initiates of Israel upon "Mount Sinai"—though for the instructed reader many other passages of like information are to be found in both sections of the Sacred Law, as also elsewhere.

To pass to a less abstruse and more elementary point, those who seek to become real initiates and aspire to the work upon the mountaintops that is feasible only to such, must first conform themselves to the Law of the Mount. That law may be so called because it involves a loftier teaching and a totally different order of conduct from those to which the uninitiated popular world conforms. We have a reference to this in the direction that a Mason's conduct ought to be such as will "distinguish and set him above the ranks of other men," and not merely leave him at their level. Hence the instruction given by the Great Master to his initiate-disciples, which is called the "Sermon on the Mount,"* and is popularly supposed

* See Matthew 5:1–7:29.—Ed.

to have been delivered upon a hillside. There exist, however, many great pieces of initiation-teaching going by that name, notably the great and eloquent discourses known as *The Divine Poemander of Hermes*; and all of them are called "sermons on the mount," not because of having necessarily been delivered upon any actual mountain, but because they relate to spiritualities and to the loftier plane of thought and action upon which every initiate must live. The "Mount" is that of initiation, where alone, in the silence of the senses, the spirit of man can learn the things of the spirit.

That the standard of thought and conduct for initiates is always beyond the capacity of the popular world is evidenced by the fact that society, however advanced in civilization, find itself quite unable to act up to it. Even the churches find the Sermon on the Mount impracticable doctrine for general social observance. It is regarded as a counsel of perfection, and eminent clerics are found declaring that it was never meant to apply to the unforeseen, complex social conditions of today, and declare that, while sound as a theoretic ideal, it must be compromised with in practice. From their low level of outlook they are right. The popular world is truly quite unable to act up to the terms of the Law of the Mount. But it is overlooked that that high doctrine was not meant for the popular world nor addressed to it. It was delivered to, and intended for, those few who have outgrown and renounced the ideals of the outer world and who seek initiation into a new and higher order of life which contradicts the wisdom of that world at every point.

But the real initiate must observe it at all cost and conflict to himself, and is told that unless his righteousness exceeds that of popular orthodoxy and convention, he cannot hope to realize the goal at which he aims. The whole life of the real initiate, and of those aiming to become such, will be at cross purposes with the standards and methods of the rest of the world, which will be as it were in conspiracy against him for not conforming to its ways; and, as with Hiram Abiff, at every attempt to leave the. gates of his temple and come into contact with the outer world, he will find himself opposed by persecuting "ruffians," by objections to his refusal to fall in with popular conventions, and by demands to know the secrets of his superiority to them. Hence one of the reasons for the silence and obscurity of real initiates, as also for Masonic secrecy, is self-protection, which the Christian Master gave as a justification for not casting pearls before those incapable of appreciating them—"lest they turn and rend you." (Matthew 7:6)

The way of the natural uninitiated man is that of self-assertion and material acquisitiveness; he is bent upon securing all he can get from this world; and wisdom, knowledge, and power, are what seem to be such in his own eyes. He is not wrong or blameworthy; he is simply fulfilling the law of his present nature, which is the only law he as yet knows; he is merely ignorant and self-blinded to any higher nature and law. The initiated man is one to whom a higher nature and law have become revealed, and who, conscious of their compulsion upon himself, has abjured all the ideals of his less advanced fellows. He lives upon the Mount and fulfills the Law of the Mount; and therefore to him come wisdom, grace and power transcending anything his uninitiated fellowmen can as yet conceive. initiates were termed by the Great Master the "salt of the earth," for, without their leavening presence in it, the world would descend to greater corruption than it at present suffers. "Ten just men (i.e., initiates) shall save the city," (cf. Genesis 18:32) as was said of those "cities of the plain" which are a figure of civilization at large.

It is not, however, for his personal aggrandizement or salvation that a man seeks, or should seek, initiation into the higher order of life, or should aspire for the wisdom and power that therewith come. To do so from this motive would be merely to imitate the ways of the outer world, apart from the fact that it would neutralize the whole purpose of initiation.

His real purpose is to help on the world's advancement, to become one of its saviors, at the sacrifice of himself. For the real
initiate is selfless; he has abandoned all personal claims and
the "rights" to which lesser men claim to be entitled; and, having crucified his own personality, is able to look upon human
life impersonally and to offer himself as an instrument for its
redemption. When wisdom and power come to him, they are
not for his own use but for the help of the whole human race;
he is a master among men, because he is a universal servant;
he is the most effective spokesman in the world, because of his
utter silence.

Masonic secrecy and silence are inculcated for this very
reason; for all spiritual power is generated in silence. In silence
the aspirant must concentrate his own energies and climb
from his own earth into his own heavens, rendering to the
Caesar of the outer world the things that are his, but in other
respects fulfilling the law of the Mount in a way that will "distinguish and set him above the ranks of other men" who are
not yet ready or prepared to follow him. If the Masonic Brotherhood has not yet risen to full appreciation of the meaning
of its own system, it nevertheless stands provided with all the
information needful to lead it to initiation in the high sense
indicated throughout these pages, to which each of its members may aspire if he follow the Ancient Sage in Tennyson's
poem and

> . . . leave the hot swamp of voluptuousness
> A cloud between the Nameless and thyself,
> And lay thine uphill shoulder to the wheel,
> And climb the Mount of Blessing, whence,
>   if thou
> Look higher, then—perchance—thou
>   mayest—beyond
> A hundred ever-rising mountain lines,
> And past the range of Night and Shadow—see

The high-heaven dawn of more than mortal day
Strike on the Mount of Vision!*

11. "From Labor to Refreshment"

The Masonic reader who recognizes that every reference in speculative Masonry is figurative and carries a symbolic significance behind the literal sense of the words, will at once dismiss from his mind any suggestion that the formula of adjourning the lodge from labor to refreshment, and of recalling it from refreshment to labor, relates to the customary practice of passing from the formal work of the lodge to the informalities of the dining table.

The familiar formula of dismissing the lodge after seeing that every Brother has received his due, no doubt came over into the present system from operative usage when guild-masons periodically received their material wages. But it has now become the *Ite, Missa est!* ("Depart, the Mass has ended!") of spiritual Masonry, and carries a sacramental meaning. We have to consider what labor, refreshment, and dues, are in their higher and concealed sense.

First as to labor. The allusion is less to the temporary ceremonial work of the lodge than to the work the earnest Light-seeker is continually to be engaged upon in his task of self-perfecting. Let it be realized that this is labor indeed, to be undertaken with earnestness and vigor. "*Hoc opus, hic labor est,*" wrote Virgil of it.† "The gods sell their arts only to those who sweat for them," runs another ancient adage of the science. Purification of the bodily senses and reformation of personal defects are but part, the simpler and grosser part, of the work; the redirection of one's mind and will to the ideal involved, the requisite research and study conducing to that end, and the necessary control and concentration of thought and desire

---

*   "The Ancient Sage" (1885), lines 277–285.

†   "There's the trouble, there's hard work." From the *Aeneid* book 6, line 126.—Ed.

upon the end in view, are not child's-play nor matters of casual, superficial interest.

Intellectual and spiritual labor necessitate rest and refreshment, equally with physical, that the harvest of that labor may be assimilated. Wise activity (Boaz) must be balanced with an equally wise passivity (Jachin) if one is to become established in immortal strength and to stand firm, spiritually consolidated and perfect in all one's parts.* Nor is it a work to be hurried; those build most surely who build slowly. *Festina lente!* "Hasten slowly!"† is an old maxim of the work addressed to those who would "lay great bases for eternity." *Ne quid nimis!* is another: "Let nothing be done in excess."‡

Now it is not easy to combine work of this nature with that which the exigencies of one's normal duties and responsibilities entail. But to those who are in earnest, the co-adaptation and harmonizing of all one's duties will form part of the work itself; one's present position and avocation will be discerned to be precisely those suited to making advancement, and to provide opportunities for doing so. Doubtless difficulty and opposition will be encountered in abundance; but these again are parts of the process and tests of fidelity. No growth is possible without resistance to draw out latent power. The aspirant must steadily and conscientiously persevere along the path to what he seeks, just as each candidate engages himself to do so in respect of its ceremonial portrayal; and every Brother may be assured of receiving his exact dues for the labor he expends.

"There is a time to work and a time to sleep." Respite from labor is as contributive an element to progress as labor

---

* An interpretation commonly found in Masonic literature is that the Temple pillars represent pairs of opposites. Scholars tend to believe the pillars had a singular significance. In Hebrew *bo'az* means "in him there is strengh" and *yakin* means "may he render firm."—Ed.

† Aullus Gellius 10.11.5. Later, it served as the personal motto of Augustus Caesar.—Ed.

‡ Terrence, *Andria*, line 61.—Ed.

itself, for the mind must digest, and the whole nature assimilate, what it absorbs. More may be learned from the teacher in the heart than from what is gathered by the head, when that teacher—the principle at the center—is once awakened. Meditation and reflection are of greater instructiveness than book-reading and information acquired from without oneself.

> Thinks't thou among the mighty sum
>> Of things for ever speaking,
> That nothing of itself will come,
>> That we must still be seeking?

For the care and nourishment of the outer body, Nature provides a passive, sympathetic system, which arranges digestion, distributes energy, builds up the body, and discharges its functions for us without interference with our formal consciousness. In like manner, in our higher being resides a corresponding principle which winnows out thought, clarifies and arranges ideas, and settles problems and difficulties for us, in entire independence of our formal awareness. It is this higher principle that must be found, trusted and relied upon to participate in the work of interior up-building. The old writers call it the Archaeus, or the hidden Mercury, which ingarners and utilizes the fruit of our conscious efforts, building them up into a "superstructure" or subtle body. As ages have gone to the organization of the physical body, so also long periods are requisite for that of the super-physical structure, the building of which is true Masonry; but the process can be expedited by those who possess the science of it, as Masons are presumed to do. The process itself is the real Masonic "labor"; and, as we have shown, it has its active and its passive aspects.

This is a difficult subject to treat of briefly. Its nature is merely indicated here, and its fuller study must be left to individual research and, where possible, to personal tuition; for this work is precisely that about which a Master Mason is presumed to be able to give private instruction to brethren in the inferior degrees.

Let the reader reflect that Masonic "labor" involves the making of his being whole and perfect; that it is intended to "render the circle of it complete." His complete being is likened, in geometrical terms, to a circle—the symbol of wholeness, entirety, self-containedness. But let him remember that as he knows himself at present, he is not a circle, but a square, which is but the fourth part of a circle. Where are the other three-fourths of himself? For until he knows these as well as the fourth part which he does know, he can never make the circle of his being complete, nor truly know himself.

This is the point at which Masonry becomes mystical Geometry—the important science of which Plato affirmed that no one should enter the Academy where true philosophy and ontology were to be learned, until he already was well versed in that science. For in former times these deeper problems of being were the subject of geometrical expression, and echoes of the science remain to us in our references to squares, triangles and circles, and particularly in the 47th problem of the first book of Euclid, which is now the distinctive emblem of those who have won to Mastership. How many of those who now wear that emblem, one wonders, have any conception of its significance? It is a mathematical symbol representing, for those who can read it, the highest measure of human attainment in the science of reconstructing the human soul into the Divine image from which it has fallen away. No wonder the great initiate who composed this symbol was raised to an ecstasy of joy on realizing in his own being all that it implies, depicts, and demonstrates, and that upon that fortunate occasion he "sacrificed a hecatomb of oxen"—an expression the meaning of which, like the symbol itself, must be left to the reader's reflection, for these matters cannot be summarily or superficially explained. Pythagoras himself is said to have re-

fused to explain them to his own pupils until they had undergone five years' silence and meditation upon them. Those
five years represent the period that is still theoretically allotted
to the work of the Fellowcraft degree, in regard to which the
modern Mason is instructed to devote himself to reflecting
upon the secrets of nature (i.e., his own nature) and the principles of intellectual truth, until they gradually disclose themselves to his view and reveal his own affiliation to the Deity. In
declining to explain these geometrical truths to students until they had familiarized themselves with them for five years,
the meaning of the great teacher of Crotona was that, by that
time, the earnest disciple would have discerned their import,
and gone far to realize it, for himself.

Labor, understood in the sense here defined, and Refreshment after it, constitute a rhythm of activity and passivity; a
rhythm similar to that which we daily experience in respect
of waking and sleeping, working and resting. To speak of Refreshment, however, in the deeper sense implied in Masonry
is even more difficult than to speak of the philosophical labor;
for it involves a subject to which few devote deep thought—the
subjective side of the soul's life as distinct from the objective
side which, for most men, is the only one at present known to
them. In that deeper sense, refreshment implies what Spenser
speaks of in the lines:

> Sleepe after toyle, port after stormie seas,
> Ease after warre, death after life does
>   greatly please. [*]

To the wise, the study of the subjective half of life is as
important as that of the objective half, and without it he cannot make the circle of his self-knowledge complete. Even the
observant Masonic student is made aware by the formula used

[*] Edmund Spenser, "The Fairie Queen" (1590), book 1, canto 9, lines 59-
360.—Ed.

at lodge-closing, that by some great Warden of life and death each soul is called into this objective world to labor upon itself, and is in due course summoned from it to rest from its labors and enter into subjective celestial refreshment, until once again it is recalled to labor. For each the "day," the opportunity for work at self-perfecting, is duly given; for each the "night" cometh when no man can work at that task; which morning and evening constitute but one creative day of the soul's life, each portion of that day being a necessary complement to the other. Perfect man has to unify these,opposites in himself; so that for him, as for his Maker, the darkness and the light become both alike.

The world-old secret teaching upon this subject, common to the whole of the East, to Egypt, the Pythagoreans and Platonists, and every College of the mysteries, is to be found summed up as clearly and tersely as one could wish in the *Phaedo* of Plato, to which the Masonic seeker is referred as one of the most instructive of treatises upon the deeper side of the science. It testifies to the great rhythm of life and death above spoken of, and demonstrates how that the soul in the course of its career weaves and wears out many bodies and is continually migrating between objective and subjective conditions, passing from labor to refreshment and back again many times in its great task of self-fulfillment. And if Plato was, as was once truly said of him, but Moses speaking Attic Greek, we shall not be surprised at finding the same initiate-teaching disclosed in the words of Moses himself. Does not the familiar Psalm of Moses (*cf.* Psalm 90) declare that man is continually "brought to destruction," that subsequently a voice goes forth saying "Come again, ye children of men!" and that the subjective spiritual world is his refuge from one objective manifestation to another? What else than a paraphrase of this great word of comfort is the Masonic pronouncement that, in the course of its task of self-perfecting, the soul is periodically summoned to alternating periods of labor and refreshment? It must labor, and it must rest from its labors; its works will follow it, and in the subjective world every Brother's soul will receive its due for its work in the objective one, until such time as its work is completed and it is "made a pillar in the House of God and no more goes out" (Revelation 3:12) as a journeyman-builder into this sublunary workshop. "Did I not agree with thee for a penny?" (Matthew 20:13) said the Great Master parabolically. Now the round disc of the coin was meant to be an emblem of that completeness, wholeness, and self-containedness which is denoted by the Circle, and which every Mason is enjoined to effect in himself. When the Mason has made the circle of his own being complete, he will not only have earned his penny and received his dues; the circle of his then glorious being will be as the sun shining in his strength, and he will be able to say with the initiates of Egypt, as they contemplated the sun ascending. from the desert into the heavens: "I am Ra in his rising!"*

12. The Grand Lodge Above

Express reference is made in the Order rituals to the existence of a Grand Lodge Above, having its Grand Master and Officers. Doubtless the allusion is often regarded as but a pious sentiment expressing the belief that, after their death, worthy Masons combine to constitute such a lodge or assembly in the heavens.

With such a belief no one would wish to interfere, but there are good grounds for suggesting that the reference was intended to carry a quite different meaning. It is meant to testify to the fact, which forms part of the long stream of esoteric tradition throughout the ages, that a supernal Masonic Assembly not only exists, but that it preceded, in point of time and constitution, the Masonic Order on earth. Had it not so existed and preceded the terrestrial Order, that Order itself would not have existed; for the hypothesis is that the latter is the shadow and projection upon the physical world of a cor-

---

* Egyptian Book of the Dead 17.1.

responding hierarchical Order in the superphysical. In other words, the Masonic Order on earth is the reflex and effect, not the generating cause, of the Grand Lodge Above. The latter is not necessarily recruited from the former, since death of the body does not constitute *per se* a title to admission to the Grand Lodge Above, which, according to the tradition, possesses its own qualifications and passports for admission; but neither, according to the same tradition, does life in the earthly body preclude the duly qualified Mason from reception into, and conscious cooperation with, the Supernal lodge, while he is still in the flesh.

A certain resemblance will be noticed between this doctrine and the corresponding theological one of the complementary relations between the "church militant" on earth and the "church triumphant" in the heavens, the doctrine of the communion possible between all saints upon whichever side of the veil. Neither in the case of the church nor of Masonry does the claim imply, what is obviously not the fact, that every member of either community has actual knowledge or first-hand experience of the truth of this doctrine. But it does imply that there have been, and still are, members possessing it.

Farther on in these pages more will be said of the Grand Lodge Above, and in a way which perhaps will suggest to the reflective reader a fuller idea than one can convey upon such a subject than by expository methods. It is a theme deserving of larger consideration than the Craft accords it, and one about which no little literary evidence is available for those with sufficient interest to look for it. One such important piece of evidence shall be mentioned here.

It consists of a remarkable series of communications of the highest spiritual value and instructiveness to every Brother seeking to realize the spiritual essence of the Masonic system, issued by a saintly man and advanced initiate, Karl von Eckartshausen, to a group of pupils in the secret science in Germany, at roughly about the same period as that in which the English Masonic Order was becoming established.* The synchronism is not without significance and, in conjunction with other evidences (which exigencies of space prevent being now adduced) of spiritual activity at work at that time behind the events of public history, points to efforts to put forward a great movement for human enlightenment; a movement conceived from behind the veil by the Grand Lodge Above, and projected into the world through some of its members in the flesh.

The communications or letters deal with the subject of the need for human regeneration and the rationale of initiation. In the first of them, the author asserts that:

> The great and true work of building the Temple consists solely in destroying this miserable Adamic hut and in erecting in its place a divine temple; this means, in other words, to develop in us the interior sensorium or the organ to receive God. After this process, the metaphysical and incorruptible principle rules over the terrestrial, and man begins to live, not any longer in the principle of self-love, but in the spirit and in the truth, of which he is the Temple. . . . The most exalted aim of religion is the intimate union of man with God; this union is possible here below, but it can only take place by the opening of our inner sensorium, which enables our hearts to become receptive of God. Therein are those great mysteries of which human philosophy does not dream, the key to which is not to be found in scholastic science.†

He then proceeds to state that:

---

* Eckartshausen's letters, with a valuable introductory essay by Bro. A. E. Waite, are contained in *The Cloud upon the Sanctuary* (W. Rider & Sons Ltd.), a work of the greatest value to Masonic students.

† *The Cloud upon the Sanctuary*, pp. 14–15.

... a more advanced school has always existed to which the deposition of all spiritual science has been confided ... which has continued from the first day of creation to the present time; its members are scattered all over the world, but they have always been united by one spirit and one truth; they have had but one science, a single source of truth, one lord, one doctor and one master, in whom resides substantially the whole plenitude of God, who also alone initiates them into the high mysteries of Nature and the Spiritual World. [*]

In the second letter it is explained (I compress the substance) that:

This community possesses a School in which all who thirst for knowledge are instructed by the Spirit of Wisdom itself; and all the mysteries of God and of nature are preserved therein for the children of light.... It is thence that all truths penetrate into the world.... It is the most hidden of communities, yet it possesses members gathered from many orders.... From all time ... there has been an exterior school based on this interior one, of which it is but the outer expression ... The community has been engaged from the earliest ages in building the grand Temple to the regeneration of humanity, by which the reign of God will be manifest. This society is in the communion of those who have most capacity for light... It has three degrees, and these are conferred on suitable candidates still in the flesh. The first is inspirationally imparted. The second opens up the human rational intellectuality and understanding, and ensures interior illumination. The third and highest is the entire opening of the inner sensorium, by which the inner man attains objective vision of real and metaphysical verities. [†]

[*]   *The Cloud upon the Sanctuary*, p. 15.
[†]   Rather loosely adapted by Wilmshurst from von Eckartshausen, pp. 26-27 and p. 10.—Ed.

The instruction goes on to explain that this Society does not resemble temporal organizations that meet at certain times and elect their own officers. It knows none of these formalities, but proceeds in other ways. The divine power is always present. The master of it himself does not invariably know all the members, but the moment a member's presence or services are needed he can be found. If a member is called to office, he presents himself among the others without presumption, and is received by them without jealousy. If it be necessary that members should meet, they find and recognize each other with perfect certainty. No disguise, hypocrisy, or dissimulation, can hide their true characteristics. No one member can choose another; unanimous choice is required. All men are called to join this hidden community; the called may be chosen, if they become ripe for entrance. Any one can look for entrance; any man who is within can teach another to seek it, but only he who is ripe can arrive inside. Worldly intelligence seeks this sanctuary in vain; all is undecipherable to the unprepared; he can see nothing, read nothing, in its interior. He who is ripe is joined to the chain, perhaps often where he thought least likely, and at a point of which he knew nothing himself. Seeking to become ripe should be the effort of him who loves wisdom. But there are methods by which ripeness is attained, for in this holy communion is the primitive storehouse of the most ancient and original science of the human race, with the primitive mysteries also of all science. It is the unique and illuminated community which possesses the key to all mystery, which knows the center and source of nature and creation. It unites superior power to its own, and includes members from more than one world. It is the Society whose members form a theocratic republic, which one day will be the Regent Mother of the whole world.

Upon this description of the Grand Lodge Above, by one who, even in the days of his flesh, claims to have been a member of it, it is not proposed here to descant. That it may provoke surprise and doubt as to its veraciousness in those to whom such ideas may now come for the first time, is probable. This must be hazarded in giving voice to those ideas here, and the subject left to such responsiveness as may come from the heart of the individual reader; for obviously no proof can either here be offered or given to even the most sympathetic querist upon a matter which in its nature is incapable of verification otherwise than by direct personal experience.

But with an earnest counsel to accept its accuracy and to seek confirmation of it in the only way in which such confirmation is possible, it must be left to the deep and protracted reflection of those to whom the idea of the existence of a Grand Lodge in the heavens, watching over the Masonic Israel on earth and superintending its development, is at least a matter of probability and a subject for faith. They will at least perceive in the description of it given above, that the Masonic Order faithfully reproduces, in point of form and hierarchical progression, its alleged supernal prototype; and if they recognize that invisible things are in some measure knowable by perceiving things that are made, the contemplation of their own three-graded Order, with its ascending sequence of Grand Lodges of districts, provinces, and finally of the nation, will perhaps help them on to the conception of an unseen Grander lodge beyond all these: one to membership of which any duly qualified Brother may hope to be called to take progressive initiations—no longer ceremonial and symbolic, but as facts of spiritual experience—at the hands of the Universal Master and Initiator, whose officers are still brethren of our own, though risen to the stature of holy angels.

Chapter Three

Fullness of Light

1. Observations & Examples

The light of the body is the eye.
When thine eye is single, thy whole body
also is full of light. Take heed, therefore,
that the light in thee be not darkness.—Luke 11:34–5

Now will I open unto thee—whose heart
Rejects not—that last lore, deepest concealed,
That farthest secret of My heavens and earths,
Which but to know shall set thee free from ills—
A royal lore, a kingly mystery;
Yea, for the soul such light as purgeth it
From every sin; a light of holiness
With inmost splendour shining.—*The Song Celestial* 9:1–2

WE have shown that initiation, in its real and not merely ceremonial sense, effects in him who undergoes it a permanent enlargement of consciousness to a level and of a quality never previously known to him. The expansion may be small or great; indeed the Science contemplates successive degrees of initiation and ever widening expansions to which no limit can be set.

The reader will ask himself, "What are the nature and characteristics of this new order of consciousness when attained? How will it differ from my present normal consciousness?" To answering this question the present paper is devoted, and it shall be dealt with first in some general observations, and subsequently in a more illustrative manner.

Even normally, and without deliberately sought initiation, human consciousness becomes enlarged as the result merely of progressive life-experience. For what is life itself but a slow, gradual initiation process, with the world as a Temple in which it is conferred? The consciousness and resultant sagacity of experienced age exceed those of raw youth, even if the change be of an intellectual rather than of a spiritual kind, and involve merely increased *savoir faire* and mundane wiliness rather than growth in unworldly wisdom. Still, enlargement has occurred, and it adumbrates what is possible with the spiritual consciousness when it becomes awakened.

Nature, indeed, exhibits nothing but consciousness in process of expansion through her fourfold series of kingdoms from the mineral upwards. The outward forms of life, even of the mineral, are but the objective bodies of a subjective life-activity resident in that body. The Earth, the planet itself, as also each of the stellar bodies, is—the Ancients rightly taught—not dead matter, but a Zôon, a living animal, conscious as a whole, conscious (though differingly) in each of its parts however materialized or tenuous, and girdled round with a zodiac of other mutually interacting "living creatures," the separate consciousnesses of all the parts of the complex mechanism blending in the synthetic Omniscience, God.

Life is fundamentally one, a unity, though distributed into many separated lives and divided into separate self-contained kingdoms, as compartments of a ship are divided by decks and bulkheads. It is "an ever-rolling stream," a stream that pours through those kingdoms in a continuous flow which is never more than momentarily checked by the forms (or bodies) it flows through, which are as it were but little eddies and vortices in the stream; and these forms, from the lowest to the most highly evolved, are devised and adjusted to raising consciousness to progressively higher levels. Nature, in a word, is a system of restricted consciousness in perishable bodies, leading up to unrestricted consciousness in an ultra-natural immortal body.

Each successive kingdom of Nature assumes into itself the sublimated characteristics of the one below it, but becomes endued with an additional principle and takes on a new and appropriate bodily form. Thus, as the scale is ascended, the sensitive, the emotional, the intellectual, and the spiritual principles are successively added and built into the evolving structure. When the Life-essence specialized in the mineral passes on into the vegetable kingdom, it, as it were, takes a degree of initiation; a fresh start is made, a new form or body is given to it as "a mark of its progress." It takes similar and higher grades of initiation, and acquires appropriate new bodies, as it passes on to the animal and thence to the human kingdoms.*

Man, as at his present evolutionary stage, is, in his lower nature, but a summary and synthesis of the three sub-human kingdoms; his embryo recapitulates, and his physique incorporates, the kingdoms he has traversed in the long ascent; but superimposed and dovetailed into it is now an additional, a spiritual divine principle, distinguishing and setting him above the lower kingdoms. To them he stands as a god; a high initiate, conscious in a way inconceivable to them. Similarly a plant is a god, an initiate, relatively to the soil it grows in; and an animal a god to the plant.

Yet in virtue of the new spiritual principle grafted upon his highly evolved bodily structure, man is capable of rising to still loftier conscious levels; he awaits still further initiation. Before him lies the prospect of outgrowing the kingdom of merely animal man and of entering the higher one of spiritual

---

* It is not here implied that mineral forms directly evolve into vegetable, thence to animal and so on, at some point which the biologist has sought for but failed to trace. This is not the case. The kingdoms of Nature are closed compartments without intercommunicating doors on the phenomenal plane, and do not there change into one another. The transition takes place on a super-physical noumenal plane, beyond the range of now current science.

Man. Four kingdoms—mineral, vegetable, animal, human—
he has known and built into his organism. He has now to rise
to a fifth kingdom, that of Spirit, of which already he is a member potentially, but without having yet developed and realized
his potencies.

The secret science therefore shows him a five-pointed star
as an emblem of himself and invests him with the five-pointed
apron as a symbol in which he may visualize himself, read his
own past, and deduce his present possibilities.

The important fact must be emphasized that, on each
transition from a lower to a higher kingdom, on each initiation into a new order of life, a death to, a complete break-away
from and abandonment of, the old form and method of life, is
involved. Natural man must, therefore, die to himself, must
abnegate and put off his old nature, before he can hope to pass
into the fifth kingdom as spiritual Man. This death, we have
shown, is signified by the Masonic third degree, which ceremonially dramatizes what the individual must pass through
before attaining an order of life and consciousness he has never before experienced or been able to experience. The death in
question is not a physical death; the physical organism is still
retained by its former wearer. He has merely effaced and died
to his old self and its natural tendencies, and suffered them
to become superseded by a new self, functioning not from his
former constricted mind, but from a new center of illimitable
conscious capacity; a capacity not displaced by the resumed
use of his physical body for the residue of its natural duration,
but one that enables him thenceforward to use that body as
a much more effective instrument for furthering the cosmic
purpose.

How is that newly-won consciousness to be described?
It is, of course, indescribable. As sight is indescribable to the
man born blind, as consciousness in this world would be un-
explainable to the unborn babe, so that of the initiate is inca-

pable of description to those as yet unborn in the kingdom of Spirit. To be known it must be experienced. It belongs to the Greater mysteries which always remain ineffable and incommunicable, whatever instruction may be imparted about the Lesser ones. Yet something may be said about it to help the imagination.

In my former volume it was explained that the moment of restoration to light in the third degree, and also the corresponding moment in the Royal Arch degree, are both of them attempts—the former a simple, the latter a more elaborate one—to dramatize the enlarged conscious state into which the candidate passes in actual initiation. A very fine and wonderful literary description of expanded consciousness effected by initiation is to be found in the eleventh section of the great Indian manual of initiation science, the *Bhagavad Gita* (most accessible to English readers in Sir Edwin Arnold's fine poetic translation, *The Song Celestial*). Dante's vision in the *Paradiso* is an example, as also that recorded in the biblical book of Revelation by the seer who was "in the spirit in the Lord's day." Keats imagined it accurately when, in *Hyperion*, he wrote of it:

> Knowledge enormous makes a God of me.
> Names, deeds, gray legends, dire events, rebellions,
> Majesties, sovran voices, agonies,
> Creations and destroyings, all at once,
> Pour into the wide hollows of my brain
> And deify me, as if some blithe wine,
> Or bright elixir peerless, I had drunk
> And so become immortal. *

A large collection of evidence and records of. personal experiences has been brought together in recent years testifying to the fact of such conscious expansions. One such compilation

---

* "Hyperion" (1819), book 3, lines 114–120.

is that entitled *Cosmic Consciousness*, by Dr. R. M. Bucke, a member of the Craft in America and an exponent of the mystical nature of Masonry. The subject has even been investigated experimentally by the late eminent psychologist Professor William James and others, and although such artificially induced heightenings of consciousness are strongly to be dissuaded from as perilous to those who undertake them—and Professor James confessed that to himself it brought with it a painful reaction and penalty—he has left an able, vivid description of what is known as "the Anaesthetic Revelation" which may be quoted; it could not better have expressed the truth had it been written by one who had attained initiation legitimately and in the natural development of the life of sanctity and contemplation, instead of by one who was merely intoxicating himself with nitrous oxide gas. He writes:

> [...in this] intense metaphysical illumination...Truth lies open to the view in depth beneath depth of almost blinding evidence. The mind sees all the logical relations of being with an apparent subtlety and instantaneity to which its normal consciousness offers no parallel.... The center and periphery of things seem to come together. The ego and its objects, the *meum* and the *tuum*, are one.
>
> ...its first result was to make peal through me with unutterable power the conviction...that the deepest convictions of my intellect hitherto were wrong. Whatever idea or representation occurred to the mind was seized by the same logical forceps and served to illustrate the same truth; and that truth was that every opposition, among whatsoever things, vanishes in a higher unity in which it is based; that all contradictions, so-called, are but differences; that all differences are of degree; that all degrees are of a common kind; that unbroken continuity is the essence of being; and that we are literally in the midst of an infinite...

It is impossible to convey an idea of the torrential character of the identification of opposites as it streams through the mind in this experience. *

With this statement let us compare one by a real initiate describing the opening up of the Light at his center:

My whole spirit seemed to break through the gates of hell and be taken up into the arms and heart of God. I can compare it to nothing but the resurrection at the last day. For then, with all reverence I say it, with the eyes of my spirit I saw God. I saw both what God is, and how God is what He is. The gate of the Divine Mystery was sometimes so opened in me that in one quarter of an hour I saw and knew more than if I had been many years at a university. I saw and knew the Being of all Beings; the Byss and the Abyss; the generation of the Son and the procession of the Spirit. I saw the descent and original of this world also, and of all its creatures. I saw in their order and outcome the Divine World, the Angelical World, Paradise, and then this fallen dark world of our own. I saw the beginning of the good and of the evil, the true origin and existence of each of them. For twelve years this went on in me. Sometimes the truth would hit me like a sudden smiting storm of rain, and then there would be the clear sunshine after the rain.

The writer of this statement was the poor, uneducated cobbler, Jacob Boehme, who lived near Dresden, and died, aged 49, in 1624, and who has been described by a disciple and competent judge as "the greatest light that has come into the world since Him who was Himself the Light of the world."† The fuller record of his illuminations and profound metaphysical

* The Will to Believe, by William James, 1897, pp. 293–294.
† Louis Claude de Saint Martin ("Le Philosophe Inconnu"); himself a Freemason and advanced illuminate.

insight can be found in his series of lengthy but difficult and obscure works, from the study of which Sir Isaac Newton, a deep student of them, drew the information from which he became able to formulate the principles of gravitation and planetary motion, and other laws now known to regulate physical phenomena.

Instances might be multiplied indefinitely of cases in which the inner being of persons ripening for initiation expands towards all sides from an infinitely deep central point in themselves, so that they acquire a totally different outlook upon life, a larger deeper envisaging of the world, than others. Three outstanding features characterize such cases. First, the fact that objects, whether those of nature or one's fellow beings, cease to be seen singly, as separate objects and beings, but as partial expressions of a single, underlying, inexpressible unity. Second, the fact that for such percipients all ordinary values become changed; what the average man supposes important shrinks to worthlessness, and what he thinks negligible assumes prime importance. Third, the fact that the five senses, distributed in the ordinary man as distinct, unrelated channels of perception, remain no longer separate and diffused, but become unified and co-functional in one comprehensive faculty, so that to see is also to hear; to touch, even with blindfold eyes, is to visualize. As a Brother in the Craft, known to me, writes of his own experience of this enrichment of consciousness: "You know everything and understand the stars and the hills and the old songs. They are all within you, and you are all light. But the light is music, and the music is violet wine in a great cup of gold, and the wine in the golden cup is the scent of a June night."

The brilliant young German, Novalis, an advanced illuminate, though he died at 29 over a century ago, tells of his Master, Werner (a professor of mineralogy at Freyburg), as one who "was aware of the inter-relation of all things, of conjunctions, coincidences. He saw nothing singly. The perceptions of his senses thronged together; he heard, saw, felt, simultaneously. Sometimes the stars became man to him, men as stars; stones as animals, clouds as plants. He sported with forces and phenomena. He knew where and how to find and bring to light this or that. What came to him more than this he does not tell us. But he tells us that we ourselves, led on by him *and by our own desire*, may discover what happened to him."

"Led on by our own desire." In desire lies the secret of it all! All initiation presupposes concentration and intensity of desire for it, and is impossible without that indispensable prerequisite. Desire turned outward, squandered upon exterior attractions, wastes the soul's forces, distributes its energies through the five channels of sense. Turned inward, focused upon interior possibilities, desire ingathers those forces, unifies those senses, and is the heat which, gathering in intensity, finds its ultimate fruition in a burst of conscious flame. "If thine eye be single thy whole body is full of light."

Here is an example. In a small lone isle of the Hebrides lived a young fisherman-crofter, one of the few natives of a place necessarily poor and with such scanty social and educational advantages that a mind of any power and depth is thrown back upon itself; a place where almost the only book is that of Nature, the only place of worship the Temple of earth and sky and sea. Such conditions, however, uninviting to most people, are particularly favorable to self-realization and initiation; since they ensure that poverty, that simplicity and unsophistication of the mind which are so difficult to acquire in crowded places and amid the tyrannies, artificialities and strife of current so-called civilization. So they were to the man in question. With something of the old primitive passion of Demeter-worship, he loved the island and the sea, his soul straining continually to know directly and at first hand the Living Beauty which he knew resided beneath its manifested veil. One golden day, in a moment of concentrated adoring contemplation, he threw himself on the ground, kissing the hot, sweet heather, plunging his hands and arms in it, sobbing the while with a vague strange yearning, and lying there nerveless, with closed eyes. His posture at that moment resembled, unwittingly yet surely, that of one who with blinded eyes and with his hands upon the Sacred Law declares that the supreme Light is the paramount desire of his heart and asks to be accorded it. And then came the moment when his longing was satisfied, when the veil was torn from his eyes and he received his initiation into light.

Suddenly—for, whatever its nature to the cold-blooded inquisition of the scientist, thus he translated the psychopathic experience he then underwent—two little hands rose up through the spires of heather and anointed his forehead and eyes with something soft and fragrant.

Thereafter he was the same, yet not the same, man; the place he lived in was the old familiar place, yet had become new, glorified. The Eternal Beauty had entered into him, and nothing that others saw as ugly or dreary was otherwise than perpetually invested with it. Waste, desolate spots became to him passing fair, radiant with lovely light. When, later, he went away to great towns and passed among their squalor and sordid hideousness, amid slums, factory smoke and grime, he saw all that others see, yet only as vanishing shadows, beneath which everything and everyone was lovely, beautiful with strange glory, and the faces of men and women sweet and pure, and their souls white.

Such was this man's involuntary initiation—unsought, or rather not knowingly sought, yet bringing him the fruits of the travail of his soul and leaving him permanently enlightened and transformed.* He came to be known among those with whom he dwelt as "the Anointed Man." In their Greek

---

* The incident is referred to in the works of the late Fiona Macleod (Wm. Sharp).

original the words "Christ" and "Christian" bore just that significance—an anointed, "baptized," for initiated man.

Actual initiation, then, regarded, as it may be, as "baptism," is of two classes, a lesser and a greater. The lesser (scripturally described as the "baptism of water") is one affecting the lower nature: the mind, the intelligence, the psychic nature and sensibilities. The mentality becomes expanded and illuminated; there is a quickening and hyperaesthesia of the senses, a growth of psychic faculty and perception; for the soul (or *psyche*) is now beginning to exercise its hitherto dormant atrophied powers.

The greater form of initiation, the "baptism of fire," is the awakening of the Spirit, the innermost essence, the "Vital and Immortal Principle" centrally resident in the soul, as the soul is resident in the sense-body. Numbers of people attain the lesser baptism in the ordinary development of life and often without awareness of the fact. The greater baptism is of rarer occurrence, and to experience it is a crisis that cannot be mistaken, or pass unnoticed or forgotten.

To attain either form, initiation of a formal character is not an indispensable requirement, for the growth of the soul, and Divine dealings with the soul, are not dependent upon human formalities. But formal initiation has always been, and is today, an opportunity and means of grace for attaining interior advancement which otherwise might not be secured and, for this reason, the Masonic initiation, though only a ceremonial one at present, assumes so great an importance and is capable of being put to uses so much higher and farther-reaching than the Craft has hitherto dreamed of.

Life itself, we repeat, serves for thousands as an initiating-process, without any supplementary formality. Numbers of people attain in less or greater measure the lesser baptism of water in the expanded consciousness associated with the poetic, artistic, musical or mystical types. Our wordsworths—Shelleys, Tennysons and the like—are natural initiates in whose lives formal initiation has played no part, and numberless unknown people exist about us who, in silence and obscurity, have developed their deeper nature and could assert of themselves:

> We have built a house that is not for Time's
>   o'er-throwing,
> We have gained a peace unshaken by pain for ever.[*]

Many there are who are conscious of the "mystic tie" that binds not merely all men into brotherhood, but all the elements of the universe into unity; who have lost the sense of separateness and divided interests that characterizes the average sensual man whose consciousness and desires extend no farther than his own carnal affections; who, still incarcerated in the mortal body can evade its prison-walls and laugh at its iron window-bars, escaping into the world of soul, exploring its wonders, mingling in conscious communion with other similarly liberated souls

> ... and there
> Spend in pure converse their eternal day
> Think each in each, immediately wise,
> Learn all they lacked before; hear, know, and say
> What this tumultuous body now denies;
> And feel, who have laid their groping hands away;
> And see, no longer blinded by their eyes.[†]

But those who know the "baptism of fire," the initiation of, and into, central Spirit, are few. To help to a conception of

---

[*]   From the "War Sonnets" of Rupert Brooke.

[†]   From "A Sonnet (suggested by some of the Proceedings of the Society for Psychical Research)" by Rupert Brooke.

such cases one may refer to recorded instances where, so fully has the Blazing Star at the human center opened itself, so habitually has its fire been brought forward into the purified carnal body and its formal mind, that that Light has become palpably visible, and not merely as a flesh-transmuting grace, beautifying and glorifying the personality, but as a radiant aura issuing from the face and person and throwing off actual quasiphysical light.

The traditional portrayal of saints and angels, surrounded by aureoles, halos and garments of flame, testifies to this advanced condition. Of such initiates as Columba and Ruysbroeck it is credibly recorded that their persons were seen bathed in self-radiated luminosity that lit up their chambers or the space around them for a wide radius. If the Central Light can so be objectified, it may be left to the imagination to surmise the intensity and range of the subjective consciousness experienced by those in whom it so burns. Such cases of "fullness of light" exemplify what is typified by the completed Temple of Solomon, into which descended the Divine Presence, flooding the whole house with its glory (2 Chronicles 7:1–3).

And now, leaving these general considerations, let us pass on to an imaginative illustration of the way in which Light in its fullness may be known and—God willing and helping—induced, by methods of actual, as distinct from ceremonial, initiation.

2. Apocalypsis
AN ALLEGORY OF INITIATION

"At the time of the end shall be vision."—Daniel 8:17

"O truly sacred mysteries! O pure Light! I am led by the
light of the torch to the view of heaven and of God. I am
made whole by initiation. The Lord Himself is the hierophant who, leading the candidate for initiation to the Light,
sends him and presents him to the Father to be preserved
for ever. These are the orgies of my mysteries. If thou wilt,
come and be thou also initiated, and thou shalt join in the
dance with the angels around the uncreated, imperishable,
only true God, the Word of God joining in the strain!"
                              —Clement of Alexandria
                              Exhortation to the Greeks 12.120

"APOCALYPSIS" is a Greek word meaning an unclothing, a
tearing away of the veils obstructing our perception of Absolute Truth. Hence our biblical word "Revelation" or "Apocalypse." The initiate-apostle Paul speaks of attaining the lofty
condition of beholding the Divine Glory with unveiled face,
reflecting it as a mirror, and becoming transformed into it in
ever increasing measure (2 Corinthians 3:18).

Whoever would thus behold and reflect naked, unveiled,
living Truth, must himself stand forth in his own naked
spirit, stripped of all obscuring veils of sense, emotion, desire,
thought. He must be, as the biblical Apocalyptist puts it, "in
the spirit" in the Lord's day, "day" implying consciousness
in the spirit (the "lord") as "night" implies the inevitable benightedness of any lower form of conscious faculty (the "servant").

In the ancient mysteries this power of spiritual perception was called epopteia, and the seers possessing it were
termed epopts. This fullness of light, this direct confrontation

of the naked human spirit with the unveiled universal Holy Spirit, was attained only by high initiates; it was the ultimate ripened fruit of initiation. "If thine eye be single, thy whole body shall be full of light." (Matthew 6:22)

What now follows is a descriptive example of the path leading to that attainment, for I desire to convey to my brethren, however feebly, an idea of what real, as distinct from merely ceremonial, initiation involves and leads to, and in no other way can I do it.

Greatly daring, therefore, I am venturing to follow—at whatever distance—the example of the initiate poet, Virgil, in the sixth Aeneid, where, in veiled terms, is portrayed the quest of the human soul for its "Father" or divine paternal principle, as that quest is there shown pursued from this dark earthly cave into the bright Elysian fields of the Universal Spirit; and also the similar, though differently expressed, examples of initiation and *epopteia* provided for us in the biblical book of Revelation, and by Wolfram von Eschenbach and Richard Wagner in *Parsifal.*

Although written in the first person, I beg that my description will be construed impersonally as regards the writer. But it is also hoped that the reader will earnestly look forward to some such experience becoming one day true of himself; not necessarily in precisely this form, but in its essential characteristics; for the Spirit bloweth where and how it listeth, and those who are taught of it may receive their lesson in differing ways, yet with uniformity of result.

How far that which follows is allegory, how far it is the work of a constructive imagination building upon preacquired knowledge, how far it voices personal intuition and spiritual experience, need not be indicated; it contains elements of each. All that matters is that it should faithfully *illustrate* truth; and those who have followed me so far and found any echoes of verity in earlier pages, will not regard me as wishing at this final stage to speak to them otherwise than with the tongue of good report and golden truth, and in terms and tones of utter-most sincerity. Whether what now is written voices truth, let him that hath understanding and inward hearing, hear and judge.

I.

Being of an inquiring disposition, hearing that in the Brother-hood called Masonic there were to be known certain valuable *arcana* and secrets of life not learnable elsewhere, and imag-ining it to be desirable from other motives which, while not mercenary, were perhaps of little better character, I followed a fashion of the time and the example of some friends, and as-sociated myself with a community from which I looked to be-come possessed of some special but undefined wisdom within a brief space of time.

Looking back now across the years, my conduct at that time strikes me as not a little unworthy. I was looking for something for nothing. I was expecting to acquire valuable knowledge without paying or working for it; to get without giving. Nor had I considered to what use I should put the ac-quisition when I had secured it. But I was young, inexperi-enced, unreflecting, and knew no better.

My presumption soon received its appropriate penalty, for on being formally and with a most cordial welcome re-ceived into the community and solemnly undertaking to con-form to its regulations, I was promptly cornered and humili-ated. Instead of being given what my rashness had expected, I was asked what I was prepared to give for the benefit of any of the brotherhood who might need it. I felt trapped, but it would have been impolite to say so. It was as obvious to them as it was painfully conscious to myself that my financial and intellectual poverty was such that I had nothing whatever to give. I was impelled, however, to mutter the perhaps scarcely sincere reply that had I been a person of any means I would have gladly contributed accordingly; an answer which, to my surprise, satisfied them, and they generously proceeded to tell me that, though I could offer them nothing, they would proceed to give *me* something, but upon the understanding that if I ever met anyone as poor as myself I must remember the present occasion, be as good as my word, and treat him liberally. The incident impressed me, and is of importance in view of later developments; for I am now trying to fulfill that old promise.

In my novel, flurried position, I had but a hazy notion of what then occurred or of what they gave me. I remember some talk about a stone, a foundation-stone, and of identifying myself with that stone and putting it to some good use or other. I did not recall any stone changing hands or passing into my possession; but then, if I were already identified with it, it would not change hands; I already possessed it and was merely made aware of something of which I was previously unconscious.

Be that as it may, on returning home I found myself in possession of a small stone which I valued as a memorial of the occasion and as a token that I was now a member of the community of which I had heard so much and had been so eager to join. My fellow members also, I found, each possessed a similar stone and were all very proud of it. It served as a passport or means of introduction when they traveled for pleasure or business. Some of them wore it openly as a pendant to their watch-chains or had it set in a ring with a square and compasses engraved upon it, or mounted as an ornament for their wives. Personally I preferred not to advertise the possession of my own stone and kept it in my pocket.

For years I carried it about with me and went my usual way in the world and attended to ordinary business. I continued to attend meetings of the community and to enjoy the company and conviviality I there met. So seductive were these that for long I did not realize that I was learning nothing of any vital use, and that the wisdom I had hoped to learn never reached me. Moreover, I did all that seemed required of me in the way of learning the work of the Society and discharging any task that was given me, yet in no way was I any different or better a man for belonging to it than I might have remained had I never entered it. No knowledge of any value, no secrets or mysteries of any moment, ever reached me, or seemed to be possessed by my fellows. Perhaps after all there were none to impart, or if there were, they did not matter.

The position, after reflection, began to feel a little absurd. I thought of ways of relieving myself of it, by resignation or discontinuing my interest in the Craft, especially as no one I consulted was able to throw me any light upon the reason of its existence. Once, while so brooding, I took the little stone from my pocket and slowly turned it over and over, my memory wandering back to the moment when I had received it. I said to myself, "I have been expecting bread, and been given a stone— this stone." Somehow it seemed to have increased somewhat in size, to have become unaccountably heavier. And then, as I scrutinized it, I detected for the first time some minute markings upon it, too small to decipher without the aid of a magnifying glass. Applying such a glass I found inscribed upon the stone the minute words "Free and Accepted Masonry"; then the Latin words *Descendit e coelo*, "it comes from heaven"; and finally, in Greek lettering, the words "Know thyself!"[*]

I pondered much upon these words and tried to realize their significance, though to little purpose. I made it in my way to see some of my brethren and sought permission to examine their stones. To my surprise, in each case I found the same inscription, though they themselves had not discerned it. It was often very faint and in some cases nearly worn away, but there on every stone it was. I pointed it out to some of them. They were momentarily interested, but then fell to talking of other things and thought no more about it. One or two seniors, of

[*] The quoted words are inscribed on the foundation stone of Freemasons' Hall, London, laid on May Day, 1775.

high rank and many decorations, grew almost angry at the suggestion that their stone exhibited anything with which they were not already fully conversant; so with them I did not press the matter. No one that I interrogated could give me any helpful explanation.

I was referred to libraries and given the loan of historical and archaeological books. I visited the headquarters of the community and there interviewed antiquaries and other learned and dignified people, but though for some years I strove diligently to trace the meaning, nothing of real value was forthcoming.

Meanwhile my stone grew gradually larger, heavier; and, as it did so, its inscription became correspondingly more visible and as if demanding more and more insistently to be read and understood. In a twofold sense it weighed upon me; its physical weight was becoming a burden, its unsolved problem an oppression to my mind. How could I get rid of it?

I happen to have a good friend or brother to whom, in emergencies, I have learned to repair for guidance. I don't know who he is, but he is extremely reliable, and though not very communicative and apt to be slow, even sullen, in his replies, and then to answer me in riddles and indirect ways, he has never once misled me. Like my puzzling stone, he too, seems somehow to be identified with myself. A medical man or psychologist would say, of course, that he was my own subliminal or supraliminal consciousness. It matters not which. I only know that he is intimately associated with me, that he has an extraordinary intuitive knowledge of myself and my personal problems, and can settle for me matters which my brain and reason do not and cannot. I have come to call him, as I find Oriental psychologists do, the Teacher or Master in the heart.

To him I referred the matter and sought his guidance. For a long time there was no answer. I tried again and again, and eventually, as my anxiety increased, his aloofness and silence diminished somewhat. But, as usual, his responses were disconnected and enigmatic; mere hints rather than explanations; as though he wished the onus of finding what I sought to know to remain with myself and that I must worry out my own solution with a minimum of help. Piecing together his fragmentary replies, they may be translated and condensed thus:

> "You cannot cast away your stone. It is yourself. You cannot evade it and its responsibilities by resigning or remaining absent from the Brotherhood in which you first acquired the stone. Once a Mason, always a Mason: in this world and in worlds to come. You stand solemnly and eternally covenanted, not only to yourself and your Brotherhood, but to the Eternal Sacred Law, to proceed with your Masonic work to the end. That Law does not permit you. to stultify an obligation deliberately made upon it, even if made ignorantly. *Ignorantia legis neminem excusat.* There may be that in you which was not ignorant, and that guided you to undertake that obligation. *Descendit e coelo.* Know thyself!"

Brooding upon this I realized in my conscience the force and truth of the advice, and that the stone and myself were now more closely identified than ever. It was the inseparable symbol of myself. It was my "stone of destiny," like the *Kaaba* or sacred Cubical Stone of the Muslims at Mecca; like the *Lia Fail* in Westminster Abbey upon which Jacob is said to have slept and kings are crowned; both of them stones, moreover, about which the legend runs that they "descended from heaven." Curious that that legend should now coincide with the inscription on my own stone! Yet what have Jacob and coronations to do with me, or I with them? "Know thyself!" Yes, indeed; for assuredly there may be unplumbed depths and unreached heights of me that my conscious mind does not yet know. But how to reach and investigate them? How is it possible to know more of myself than I do already? That was my problem.

Thus, baffled, I put the matter by for a while, or rather tried to, but it would not permit itself long to be ignored. The stone continued so to grow in bulk and weight as to become well nigh as unportable as its meaning grew increasingly intractable.

Ultimately, one day, in despair, I carried it out into a lonely moorland wilderness with the intention of finally grappling with its mystery and unraveling it once and for all, or of leaving it there ... if I could. As I went I remembered Bunyan's Pilgrim, carrying on his back the intolerable pack which fell away of itself when he reached the top of a certain hill. I half hoped similar relief might befall myself, but did not expect it. I had again earnestly appealed to my inward monitorial friend for further succor; but this time he had not answered at all.

Weary in body, distraught in mind, I bore my burden, now grown to a weight I could barely carry and finally pitched it down among the ling and bracken of the heath, and in the evening dusk flung myself down to rest, and upon the stone— my stone of destiny—pillowed my head, and from exhaustion fell asleep.

II.

I slept, but my heart waked.*

Though asleep I did not wholly lose consciousness, but retained a pleasurable feeling of knowing I was asleep, that my fatigued body and brain were at rest, and myself, my released and quickened intellect, was free to act in independence of them. Oh, the rest and blissfulness of that conscious sleep!— paradoxical as it may sound.

Though I knew my tired head and harried brain rested upon the hard stone, that hardness presently seemed to be dissolving and the pillow to become one of the softest down,

---

* An allusion to Song of Songs 5:1.—Ed.

swathed in fine linen, most white, most cool, lavender-scented. Yes, and more; it became vibrant; intensely, healingly vibrant. Sweet scents exhaled from it; but also sound—oh!—gorgeous strains matching the delicate fragrance, welling sweetly, softly, from afar; the twain perfectly concordant; unisoned rather; odor melodious, incense musical!

Presently, in this intensifying joy, my eyes opened. It was no longer dusk. Soft golden light was everywhere, through which pulsed now and again, like summer lightning, throbs of rosy and other colored rays of more than rainbow purity, while the ground about me, upon which I lay, was no longer the rough moorland, but fleecy down of most restful violet hue, as though one had passed through the dark-blue vault of the night-sky and lay upon the sunlit upper side of it.

I raised myself and looked round. Standing near me I saw one whom, instantly and instinctively, I recognized as my hitherto unseen friend and brother, the concealed interior monitor, to whom I had previously addressed my appeals for counsel. What a mighty, glorious being he was as he stood there, a dazzle of flame-like hair circling his fine head, his feet also winged with wreathing harmless fire; his person white-robed with a garment that seemed, not put on, but to grow from and be an integral part of him, and about his neck and loins the shimmering blue and gold clothing of—to my amazement—a Grand Lodge Officer. In one hand he bore a tall crystal wand like a deacon's, and his other arm held a golden *thyrsos* or caduceus.

We both smiled a recognition when our eyes met. I discerned that he was waiting there till I was sufficiently rested.

"Where are we?" I asked.

"In the *Aula Latomorum!*"

"Freemasons' Hall!" My thought translated his words, and then as swiftly ran on by habit, "Great Queen Street, London, WC2. But surely not there!" And I saw that his mind read mine though I spoke not.

"No, not there. That is far below you now; far removed, yet not so much by distance as by difference of conscious state."

"Then where am I?"

"In the candidate's preparing-room of the *Aula Latomorum*; the Supreme Universal lodge of all Builders in the Spirit; what you have heard of as The Grand Lodge Above."

I began to protest that I was unfitted for, and had no title to admission to, such a place, but he checked me, saying: "You have sought, asked, knocked, though you did not know it. That forms your title to admission. Your search for wisdom, your continued askings for light, did not pass unobserved by the Eye that watches here, that never slumbers nor sleeps. Your blind strivings after truth were heard as knocks upon our door, and for you that door will now open. You are being awaited within. Come, we will enter the lodge!" And he placed a gentle but powerful arm around me.

I still hesitated, but the bracing vitality of his presence and touch counteracted my weakness and gave me tenseness and courage. Nevertheless, as we began to move away, I turned and looked back upon my sleeping body in the gloom at my feet, with its head couched upon the rude dark stone—the poor, poor rags of myself. From it, linking me with it, I saw issuing a slender silvery streak, a phosphorescent filament faintly visible against its violet background.

"That," said my guide, "is your cable-tow, by which you shall be restored later on to the blessing of your material comforts: if, indeed, comforts they be to you," he added with a laugh. "They *are* a blessing, nevertheless, for without them you could never have reached or entered here. Now come!"

"What is that glorious music?" I asked, as we passed up a great stairway, the steps of which his fire-winged feet scarcely touched. For its tones grew louder, richer, as we ascended, and its waves rolled out upon me like ocean billows.

"Pending your arrival, the Grand Organist is playing selections from the Music of the Spheres for the healing of your bruised spirit. The fragrant music your stone pillow echoed back to you just now was its overtones. This lodge, the heavens, yes, and the earth beneath, are all built and held together by that music, though few of you in the world below have ears to hear it."

So we passed on.

III.

We reached the first landing of the vast Hall. It was quadrangular, and flanked at each side by a corridor by which one could perambulate the building. My guide conducted me along the four sides.

"This," he told me, "is the floor upon which labor all Architects in the Spirit under the guidance of the Universal Great Architect. There are two higher floors; one for the Geometrician who issue the designs for the Architects to fabricate into shape; upon the other labor those still greater souls who are in the secret counsels of the Most High and dwell within His shadow."

We reached the portal of a central hall, the Lodge-room of the great Apprentice Architects. Without it stood a great being bearing a sword that flashed every way, but observing my clothing and condition, he let it fall and asked in whose name I sought admission. And with a ringing voice, like a silver trumpet, my guide replied for me.

"In the name of the Son of the Carpenter, the Grand Carpenter of the universe of worlds and men, by whom all things are made!"

And, as the great gates opened, from within, upon rolling waves of sound, welled forth the antiphon "Hallowed be that name to everlasting. His kingdom come, without as here within!"

So we entered.

I may not tell all that I saw or that occurred in that wondrous place, that great assembly. But this I will tell, that at one

place I found myself before two interlaced triangles of lighted candles, three of which were lesser and three were greater
lights, and at their center, making seven, stood still another
light, the greatest of them all and of brilliance so intolerable
that I was constrained to fall upon my knees before the candlesticks and shield my eyes from their light with both my hands.
Thus kneeling, self-blinded, words were spoken to me that can
never be repeated but that seemed to proceed from the central
great candle. And presently I was asked if, voluntarily and of
my own free will, I would enter into a great and solemn covenant with the Voice speaking from it, which covenant would
not be formulated for me but, as a test of my sincerity and
desire, must come as the spontaneous prompting of my own
heart. And then, in my ignorance, simplicity and blindness,
but under my compelling joy at the wonders that even so far I
had witnessed, I behaved as a child who has been shown some
new thing that delights it and forthwith must necessarily run
away to tell the tidings to its friends. And I exclaimed that
thenceforward never would I conceal from anyone in the world
the unimaginable splendors that lay so near it yet passed un-
perceived, but that on the contrary I would reveal them to all
men and as far as possible make everyone know about them,
and that of the light and bliss in which I stood bathed I would
carry back so much into the dark world that no one should fail
to see it, and that if needs be I would be content to be ground
to dust and cast far and wide in sparklets of powdered light, if
by so doing that light might be more widely diffused.

While I still spoke my hands were drawn from my eyes
by another hand, which then took one of mine, and the Voice
said: "Rise, brother with the child's heart; of such is this kingdom. Be thou my candle-bearer, and let there be Light!"

I was raised from my knees, but, rising, my mind seemed
to rise in correspondence, to widen out enormously in its
perceptions and conceptions as the result of something that
thrilled into me from the touch of that hand. All I had before

seen and understood seemed but as darkness to what I now saw, and I, who in my impulsive ignorance had said I would become the light of the world, now beheld the great central candle-light of the seven to be no longer a candle, but to be He who Himself bears that name.

"*Domine, non sum dignus!*" * Again I would have fallen to my knees, but the Great Benignity, the Hierophant who walked among the candlesticks, restrained me and, for my support, drew a garment as it were of pure white lambskin from the substance of His own person, in which garment and flesh were one, and girded it about my loins as an apron, saying:

"This is My Body, given for you, that your body may be given for Me." And again waves of colored sound poured over me from choired voices singing "*Ecce Agnus Dei, qui tollit peccata mundi!*" †

And a great strength passed into me, so that all weakness fled and I stood erect before Him, an accepted Apprentice Mason of the Grand Lodge Above.

Then gathering into His hand the three lesser lights, they blended there into one another and became one light, one candle, which He placed in my hand, bidding me light my way with it until such time as I came to the measure of perfect man and the high stature of a Master Mason, and thereafter to go forth with it to them that sit in darkness and the shadow of death.

When, amid swelling music, my guide led me forth from that great hall, its vast assembly rose to salute their new brother, passing before them, bearing his lighted candle. And thereafter I was free to enter their abodes and workshops where I was shown the work and the methods of those who are indeed the constructive builders and carpenters of everything in the world of manifested form, from the fabrication of a solar system to that of the bodily organisms of all that inhabits it, from

*   "Lord, I am not worthy!"
†   "Behold the lamb of God, who takes away the sins of the world!"

the building of a planet to the manufacture of the simplest mechanism of human invention; for what is such an "invention" but a discovery, a finding out, and "coming upon" by the human mind of something of which the pattern already exists upon an, at present, concealed ultra-human level? Here were visible and exposed the secrets and mysteries in regard to all created forms and physical phenomena. Here the forces constituting natural law were controlled and regulated; here continents, oceans and waterways were planned, and human racial distribution prearranged. In this department worked those who devised the constitution of states, kingdoms and polities for the lower world; in that, those who compiled tables and codes of law for social use and government, plans of ethical systems, religious, ceremonial and sacramental forms for human use and educating human understanding in celestial truths. And among these latter were to be seen the originals of the great systems of ritual and symbolism devised to train the human eye and imagination to the perception of spiritual principles to which otherwise they would remain blind—such as those of the Hebrew and the older Christian churches, the ancient schools of the mysteries, and also modern Freemasonry, the source of which, so nebulous and uncertain to terrestrial research, here becomes crystal-clear. For all such institutions exist in the outer world, not from chance compilation or unaided human ingenuity, but because they are "patterns of heavenly things," physicalized reflections of preexisting fabrications by Architects and Workmen laboring Upon a loftier and more enlightened plane of being than that of the flesh, a plane from which they become inspirationally transmitted to the minds of those below or to which some such minds are able consciously to mount and receive direct instruction; as did the Hebrew initiate, Moses, when enjoined to frame the religio-political system of his people and in doing so to "see that he did all things in accordance with the pattern shown him in the Mount." (Hebrews 8:5)

For in this celestial "Mount" are made all the patterns or models of whatever is good, useful and worthy in the terrestrial "valley" below, where nothing is really *made*, but merely copied and reproduced. From here the prophet, the poet, the artist, the musical genius, the inventor, wittingly or unwittingly draw all the conceptions that become the heritage of man and help on his racial career, but that at the same time convey to him an illusory sense of self-generated progress and a belief in his own cleverness.

Thus was I made free of the great brotherhood of the Supernal Architects, working without haste, without rest, in the world of Light. Yet my thought reverted to the builders in the dark world below, where, if they can build nothing other than their own good or evil destiny,

> All are architects of Fate,
> Working in these walls of Time...
> Broken stairways, where the feet
> Stumble as they seek to climb. *

But my flame-shod guide beckoned me, and, remembering that before I could carry light into that tenebrous realm I must go on to the measure of perfect man, I followed him.

IV.

He led me forth and up a great winding stairway to the next landing of the vast Hall, to the Lodge of the Geometricians, and twice was I conducted around its galleries as though the better to adjust myself to that loftier plane of being. Presently, after due preparation and carrying my candle as passport, I was granted admission to its central chamber. And there the Hierophant, whom previously I had met as the Great Archi-

* Henry Wadsworth Longfellow, "The Builders" (1850), lines 1–2 & 27–28.

tect, now manifested to me in a different and higher guise, as the Grand Geometer.

Now He stood in the midst of a triangle of three great lights, and presently these, too, He gathered into His hand where they blended into one which He placed in my other hand, so that now I stood bearing a pair of candles, one a lesser light that shone but as the moon, and one a greater that blazed as the sun shining in his strength. And I was made to know that I should need both these lights upon the path that still lay before me.

And when the greater light was placed in my hand my previous illumination seemed but as moonlight in comparison with that which now came to me, and what had up to that moment seemed to me vacuous space I now perceived to be thronged with an innumerable concourse of great beings greeting me into their company, each holding a hand high aloft and chanting over me in chorus: "Sun, stand thou still in his heights; and moon, stand thou still in his valleys, until all his enemies be overcome in the great day of his perfecting!"

And the Great Initiator placed his hand within his own bosom and drew forth a chalice of red wine and, holding it forth to me, said, "This is My life-blood, given for you that yours may be made Mine. Take, drink!"

And I drank, and gave thanks, and was dismissed to pursue my way.

Hitherto I had perceived as it were with but outward sensible eyes, and had gazed upon but the outward forms and surfaces of what I saw. Now, at this draught of new wine, my inward intellectual eyes became opened too, penetrating beyond all forms, beholding their animating essence; seeing not separate existences and objects, but all life, all objects, in inseparable unity. Here was what Socrates so rapturously tells of in Plato's Phaedrus—and I knew that, to tell it, he too must have been called to this same place and been granted this same measure of initiation—that it is a region of which no earthly bard has ever yet sung or ever will sing in worthy strains, one where for the:first time one comes to know *real* existence, colorless, formless, intangible, visible only by the topmost crest of the human mind, the noetic intelligence that sits at the helm of the soul and that alone can share communion with Divine Mind; that cognizes the essential substantiality, as distinct from the accidental properties and attributes of things; no longer thinking of what is just, strong, beautiful, righteous, and so on, or of any contrasted relationships, but directly beholding Wisdom, Strength, Beauty, Goodness, in their absoluteness and in their real essential being.

Here, too, I saw the prototypal "ideas" lying behind the patterns and models shown to me in the workshops of the Architects below, and realized the geometrical and mathematical principles upon which those fabrications were based, and how that every created thing is made by measure, number, and weight, as the initiates of the Pythagorean School made known to men in the outer world, so that of a verity I saw that even the hairs of our head are numbered—not in the sense of being counted, but of existing conformably with mathematical necessity—and that not a sparrow falls to the ground apart from that necessity or without recording a fact of, and a change in, the Universal Consciousness. For on this plane where, as Plato declared, "God geometrizes,"* the Divine Ideas are assimilated by the Geometricians who there labor continually, and thence are transmitted to the lodge of the Architects below for expression in concrete form. And long would I have lingered here absorbing these inexhaustible wonders, but again I remembered my pledge and my directions, and besought my guide to lead me onwards.

---

*   This statement does not exist in Plato's extant writings, but it can be found in Plutarch, *Convivialium disputationum*, 8.2.—Ed.

V.

But how shall I relate what next befell me? How voice that which is of the Silence? I had been already led through two new supernal planes of being, one devoted to the building of form, the other to formless self-subsisting principles and abstractions—the ethereal embryos conceived by the Geometers, to which it was the function of the Architects to provide objective embodiment. Now I was to pass to a height surpassing, transcending, both these; one where there existed neither the formal nor the formless, but as it were a primal Chaos from which both had issued and into which both were resolvable; a Matrix beyond thought, beyond imagination, beyond description; and while within me was a great urge of my spirit to go further forward and enter it, there yet fell upon me for the first time in that realm of bliss and peace, of color and sound, of bodily strength and mental clarity, an apprehension that the limits both of my endurance and conscious possibility had been reached, that I could neither know nor bear more than I already knew and bore, and that to attempt to advance farther was presumption and foolishness destined to end in failure and disaster.

"Let strength be perfected out of weakness!" said my guide, reading my thought. "Come, let us go up the Hill of the Lord!" (Isaiah 2:3) Once more his strong arm was around me, and holding my lesser and greater candles, my moonlight and my sunlight, in either hand, I ascended with him towards the third and topmost story of the great *Aula*.

As we mounted, the path became less and less clear; as a highway, leading into open country, terminates in a mere track which finally disappears entirely. And despite the brilliance of the two lights I carried, a twilight seemed to be descending upon us that deepened more and more around us as we rose, until, on reaching a level landing, nothing about me remained visible, or only the most shadowy outlines of what was immediately adjacent.

Although within a building, the building itself no longer appeared as such, but to have become dissolved into something different, indefinable, indescribable—mere "place," to which no epithet or attribute can be attached; no corridors, no departmental chambers, such as I had found on the floors below; no sign of life or activity, but utter desertedness and dereliction, and yet, withal, a sense that life abounded there upon all sides. Yet thrice was I escorted around what, had it been a visible quadrangle, would have been its four sides, as though to habituate myself to these new conditions.

Deep silence and solitude ruled up here in this dark polar region of the human mind, and here the great music that flooded the lower altitudes failed, it seemed, to reach, as though the air was too rarefied for it longer to be audible or my hearing too gross to respond to it. At times we seemed to be in a dense forest, to be passing beneath the dusky boughs of giant cedars of Lebanon and other mighty growths. At length I inquired of my guide what this place was.

"This," he answered, "is the House of the Sons of the Widow"; and then for the first time a mighty emotion swept through and shook even his strong frame, as he murmured, rather to himself than for my hearing, the words, "*Sub umbra alarum Tuarum, Jeheschuah!*",* as though he too longed to dwell for ever in that place of deep shadow.

And my thought turned to the remembrance of a teaching concerning the bereft Divine Wisdom, the *Sophia*, the Bride widowed through the ages of Her errant sons until, reverting from the ways of foolishness, they voluntarily return to sonship and She becomes justified of Her children.

We halted, at length, at a place at which, in the gloom, showed the outline of two pillars standing side by side, separated only widely enough for one man to pass between. From here, my guide told me, I must proceed alone, since he could accompany me no farther; but he would prepare me for my

---

*   "Under the shadow of thy wings, Yeheshuah!"

entry into that final sanctuary and would wait without until I rejoined him.

Then he began upon me a great and solemn ritual of preparation.

He took from my one. hand the great solar light it carried, and placed the candle in a sconce at the head of one of the pillars in front of me; and then took from my other hand the lesser lunar light and set its candle in a similar sconce at the head of the other pillar; repeating, the while, with intense earnestness the words: "Thou, sun, stand still in his heights; and thou, moon, stand still in his valleys, till his enemies be overcome in the great day of his perfecting!"

He divested me of all my garments, save one only—the apron with which the Great Hierophant had invested me in the lodge below. For my other garments, ethereal though they were, were as the outgrowth of my own nature, the condensed exhalations of my own thought and desire, now become objective and clinging to me as raiment; and of these I must necessarily stand denuded if spirit is to meet Spirit and, out of my flesh, I am to see God. But my apron no other hand could take from me than that which gave it, and it remained around my loins to be my strength and support in that day of my perfecting.

Then, from an overhanging tree, he plucked a feathery spray of acacia-leaf and, after weaving it into a fillet, placed it around my head, saying as he did so: "Thou art crowned in the halls of death that hereafter thou may'st wear a Crown of Life that fadeth not away."

Further, he took the golden caduceus or thyrsos he had always carried, and, standing before me, raised it aloft, as a crucifix is held before the eyes of the dying, and exclaimed:

"Receive this Golden Bough, thou branchlet of the eternal Life-Tree, and think upon it when thou hangest upon that Tree, that thou may'st become for ever grafted thereinto, and thy leaves and fruit thenceforth be for the healing of the nations!"

And by a gold cord he placed it upon me, so that it hung suspended against my flesh as a pectoral cross.

Then, with his forefinger, he sealed me at five points with the sign of the cross; upon my brow, upon my throat, upon my heart, upon the palms of both my hands, and upon both feet. And after each sealing with the cross-sign, he sealed me again at the same points with a peace-kiss, as though with his lips to heal wounds which his finger had made; and he said: "Thou art wounded in love in the house of thy friends that by love thou may'st be made whole. These be thy five points of perpetual fellowship with Love Immortal; that in love thou may'st think, may'st speak, may'st feel, may'st act, may'st walk, when thou goest forth among the sons of men."

And having thus done, he turned from me and passed to the twin pillars standing in front of me. There, kneeling between them and with a hand laid upon each, as though to unite them in himself, his voice pealed forth into the distance beyond:"In strength have I striven to establish this son of Thy House, that he may stand firm and steadfast in the great day of his at-one-ment with Thee, Most High!"

Finally, he rose, and taking his rod or wand, passed behind me, so that I saw him no more. But I felt his presence, and that from it was now issuing an energy that was directing, compelling—even propelling—me forward; an energy at once of will and of prayer, of will that absorbed and gave direction and intensity to my own will, of prayer that shielded me from all evil as that will urged me on into the valley of the shadow of death; an energy, silent, yet of such gathering intensity that, like a great sea-wave rising to the breaking-point, I knew it must at last break into sound, and that that sound would carry me forward with it.

Presently it broke. It broke upon my hearing, upon my whole being, as one great clear word of power, the vibrancy of which swept me onward. What that word was cannot be related, nor did I then understand it. But as it translated itself at that moment to my understanding, it was the heart-speech of my directing guide saying:

"Father, into Thy hands I commend his spirit, which is also my spirit!"

And, impelled by that word of power, I passed forward along the straight and narrow way between the lighted pillars, into the gloom beyond.

VI.

The ground beneath my feet rose steeply. I felt myself to be ascending a hill in that dusk and stillness, though for some distance a state of twilight remained to me; for memories and remnants of the light that had previously suffused me lingered, and the great twin candles I had borne to this point still cast helpful beams of from the pillar-tops for a little way. But the farther Light I traversed, the higher I mounted, their illumination diminished, until at length twilight melted into utter dark. I remembered and comforted myself with, a great word: "The sun shall no more be thy light by day, neither the moon by night; but the Spirit shall be to thee an everlasting light, and thy God thy glory; and the days of thy travail shall be ended."

I knew what others have recorded of passing into the Divine Gloom, the *agnosia* of the human spirit, where vision fails and thought is paralyzed, and where that zero-point of consciousness must be touched where nothing is known to be, neither one's self, nor even God; and I knew, and again tried to comfort myself with the reflection, that even this appalling darkness was in fact light, albeit light of intensity so unthinkable as, to eyes not yet opened and inured to it, to appear as darkness. But I had yet to learn that even such comforts as thought and memory provided were staffs that must fail me of support.

In that darkness I now was. In the rarefied atmosphere of
the mount I was ascending my being took on an ever-increas-
ing hyper-sensitiveness, until I felt my flesh, even the tenuous ethereal flesh of my present body, dissolving away, leaving me as but a quivering structure of exposed, unprotected
nerves. The feathery fillet of acacia-leaf upon my forehead felt
now as a heavy crown of coarse thorns clamped upon my brow,
into which the tender, delicate frond-points pressed like steel
spikes. The light gold thyrsos suspended from my neck became
as an heavy cross, beneath the intolerable weight of which,
with bleeding feet and hands, I toiled and staggered upwardly.
I paused awhile to rest and with my forefinger swept, from
time to time, the increasing blood and sweat from my brow
and in my agony cried aloud:

"Come to my help, ye Sons of the Widow! For I, too, am
the Widow's son."

But no answer, no help came; yet the oftener I lingered,
the more I faltered, the more conscious became I of the propelling urge of that mighty word of power by which my guide
had sped, and still was speeding, me upon my willing quest;
and I knew that from a distance—how far, how short, mat-
tered not—he still was watching, directing me; that his rod
and staff controlled and safeguarded me.

In the ocean-depths there is a point at which a sinking
ship can sink no farther, the pressure upon it from above and
the resistance from below so counteracting each other that
it remains suspended and undergoes disintegration by the
dual forces grinding upon it. In the ocean-depths of Universal Spirit there is a corresponding point of equilibrium, where
the human soul, seeking to pass from terrestrial attraction to
spiritual freedom, becomes caught and ground between similar upper and nether millstones. That point is the mystical
Gethsemane, literally "the place of the wine and oil press," for
there the soul reaches the equator-line where the opposing attractive forces of soul and spirit meet, and where the former

experiences to its joints and marrow a sundering of its parts. There—as wheat is winnowed from corn-stalk and chaff, as wine and oil are distilled from crushed fruit—the soul's spirit, its sublimated, refined, immortal essence, is dissected from the sheath in which it has matured, is separated and rendered free to commence a new independent life of its own, while that sheath itself is left to perish.

That Gethsemane I had now reached. My soul consciously knew the growing division of its kingdoms, "one dead; one powerless to be born;" and again and again cried in its anguish for help from the Widow's Sons, yet without avail; and at last resigned itself to the compelling word and will that it felt still to urge it forward, higher.

Beyond Gethsemane rises the Hill Calvary—*Kranion* or *Calvaria*, the bald headland, the rocky summit, of no earthly situation, and known to none save the naked human spirit which ascends to it, there to be lifted up high above all terrene ground and magnetic attraction, and pass to birth and apotheosis in the free uncontaminated air of Spirit Absolute.

Reaching that summit, my limbs failing under me, one thing alone saved me from complete collapse—the strength and support that came, that seemed newly and increasingly generated, from the apron girt about my loins. And then, from that central peak, my feet involuntarily losing touch with the supporting ground beneath, I felt myself lifted up above the earth.

No hand there was that touched or raised me. As one whose limbs become distended, rigid, under the infusion of a strong electric current, so now the charge of the *Creator Spiritus* passed into me, forcing my frame into vertical erectness and rigidity, extending my arms horizontally, making taut and tense under its strain every fiber of my being. In mid-air, my head held toward heights I could not reach, my feet down-pointing to the earth they no longer touched, my arms wide-flung transversely into void space, I hung suspended upon that invisible impalpable Life-Tree; myself a cross; myself the crucified upon that cross.

For three hours of darkness—hours not of human time, but of that Spirit to which a day is as a thousand years—I hung upon that cross, that stauros upon which, from the foundation of the world, Life Creative hangs self-immolated, that worlds may be built upon its pattern and Life Created be fashioned at last into its image.

As there I hung, my thorny crown stabbed its spikes more deeply, more insistently, into my brow, my hands unable longer to move and wipe away the blood and sweat. Yet a joy began subtly to tincture and relieve that pain, as I realized that, under the same strain that my own being knew, the life-sap of the fragile acacia-sprig was also being quickened, was pulsing fast, striving to break to golden bloom; and that, when that bloom broke, light would break for me also and my crown of thorns become a crown of life.

The gold *thyrsos* upon my breast burned itself into me, until its vertical shaft felt one with my own spinal column, from the base of which the uprising intertwined serpents were as dual streams of a new, larger, richer vitality surging upward through my nerves towards my head, where I knew that—like the dual parts of an electric current that, meeting, flash into light—they would eventually combine and flame to conscious wings, wide-spreading as those of its symbol, far-reaching as my own wide-flung arms.

And my Craftsman's apron, at once a weight and a support to my straining loins, felt growing into me, to be becoming of my very flesh and substance. I knew now why, traditionally depicted as a loin-cloth, this garment alone was worn upon the Cross by the "King of the Jews," the Supreme Chief of all initiates, and why all the great painters of the crucifixion-scene had been moved, intentionally or inspirationally, so to depict it and not otherwise, not from any paltry motive of delicacy or prudery, but to point, for those who can understand, the truth that the secret, basic, generative energies procreating the universe and regenerating human souls must ever remain beyond the ken of all but the Divine Eye.

As with the dying, my consciousness fluctuated from a negative to a preternaturally acute and vivid stage, ranging at times to a wild yet orderly delirium; yet from both these extremes I knew the necessity of holding my will oriented and fixed upon its desired goal. At times it became cosmically comprehensive; at times it would focus upon trivialities and irrelevances. At one moment it would enlarge till, for the little leaf-crown on my head, I wore vast star-belts as a diadem; great constellations filled no more space than the palms of my hands and swam around my person as but dancing fire-flies; my trunk and legs reached down through abysmal leagues of space to the dust-speck of earth below my feet. At another the heavens would open and expose their joyous contents—a lure and temptation promptly to be rejected as often as it recurred; for, though I thirsted, it was for richer wine than they could give to drink. Now each hair of my head seemed a filament and conduit linking me with angel-hosts and reservoirs of supernatural intellectuality, and now the nerves of my feet ramified into the finest rootlets and tentacles through which I became aware of the activities of nature and of life in the earth below and the minutest details of personal human interest. I heard the crackle of growing grass, the twitter of birds, the cries and laughter of children, equally clearly with the throb of engines, the activities of industry, the clash of armies. No grain of sand, or speck of dust, or cell of tissue, but disclosed its constitution, its potencies, its purpose, its destiny; all straining, striving, building, unbuilding, rebuilding; each sealed with and bearing, wittingly or not, its little cross in one universal effort to become raised to that final cross of transformation upon which I now hung, and thence to pass on to unimagined heights and destinies beyond. Even my Brother builders in the symbolic Craft—for

of them too I became vividly aware in their little dark circum-
scribed world below—there they were in their lodges, reeling
off memorized rituals, correcting one another at a wrong or
misplaced word supposed to affect the efficacy of their work;
and some were in banquet halls, and, amid the pop of cham-
pagne corks, I heard them toasting one another, extolling the
virtues of Masonry, shouting, "Prosper the Art!" and singing
of the "mystic tie" that—more truly than they know—binds
all together and advances the building of a Temple conceived
of as yet by but few of them.

Darkness, over-intensified, at last of itself becomes as
it were a pleasurable light; pain, when ability to feel it is ex-
hausted, a measure of joy; for these opposites are but rela-
tive, the poles of a single fact; differing reactions to enforced
environment. But neither such light nor such joy was that
I longed for. They belonged to feeling, to desire, to thought;
not to that deeper factor, the Spirit, which transcends them
all, and to which I strove to keep my will one-pointed. But at
length feeling died in me; I knew neither pain nor joy. Then
desire died; what happened further to me, good or ill, I cared
not. Lastly, thought died also; its flickerings and veil-wisps
gradually falling away, till stark blankness only remained.
Nothing of me still was, save the laboring spirit that strove to
be born but could not. It was the zero-point of negative consciousness, the moment of the apparently everlasting NO;
where nothing is, and God is not.

Eloi, Eloi! Lama Sabachthani! (Psalm 22:1)

VII.

I revived—yet not I—at length, in Light; a new indescribable
light, so much more than light because it is also life; life beyond the category of personality; life in the Universal Spirit of
light:

Light rare, untellable, lighting the very light;
Beyond all words, descriptions, languages! *

The sprig of acacia had at last burst to golden flower upon
my head.

No tongue may or can speak, nor pen write, of that "sleep
in Light" as the Egyptian records call it, that conscious rest of
the soul in God, that identic union between finite object and
infinite Subject, that nirvanic absorption of the spirit's still
flame within the Fire of Divine Mind, of the human water-
drop in the ocean of that Immaculate Illimitable which is
Nothing, but without which nothing is—that impersonal yet
self-consciousness which becomes possible only when every
activity of sense and emotion has been quelled, every energy
of the restless mind stilled, all thought obliterated; and the
babe-soul rests upon the naked bosom of that Spirit of which
it has been well written:

I am the Silence that is more than Sound.
If therewithin thou lose thee, thou art found!
The stormless, shoreless Ocean, which is I—
Thou canst not breathe, but in its bosom drowned! †

What previously had seemed utter darkness was now a
sea of softest light thronged with life; living light, lighted life.
About me thronged the uncountable Sons of the Widow, God's
Master Masons, the Lords of Wisdom and sharers of the secret
counsels of the Most High, whose inspirations, transmitted to
the Geometers and Architects upon the planes below, dictated
the plans upon which worlds are built, maintained, dissolved,
and yet are but as foam upon the rising and falling waves on
the surface of the Universal Life-stream.

*   Walt Whitman, "Prayer of Columbus," lines 43–44.
†   James Rhoades, "Out of the Silence," lines 13–16.

And these great Sons, close present to me through my long agony, but invisible till a deeper sight was born in me that could share their intenser light, took me down from my cross—but of the secrets and mysteries that thereupon became known to me I do not here speak, nor of the still higher grades of initiation that lie beyond that I now testify to. When eventually I left them, I passed through their ranks, as I had passed through them upon my arrival when to my unperfected eyes they had appeared as a vast forest of Libanus cedars under whose swarth boughs I had walked; for were they not as great trees crowning the mountain-top of the world, diffusing over it from their spread branches the dark actinic rays of a Wisdom not yet recognized by men's imperfect vision as Light? I rejoined my former brother and guide at the point where I had left him, between the pillars. Upon seeing me he at once greeted me with a familiar sign in sympathy with my now vanished sufferings, and, kneeling, at the next moment shielded his eyes with his hand as my presence dazzled him with the light it now radiated. Then he rose, and bowing, drew near me and offered me his hand as a Brother of the Third degree in that Grand Lodge, and as we embraced he exclaimed:

"The Master is risen!"

And I to him responded: "He is risen indeed!"

And we passed back down the grand stairway, up which he had previously brought me, now no longer deserted, but thronged with Geometricians and Architects come forth to hail their new Brother, now journeying back as a light-bearer into outer dark world. And, upon rolling organ-music once more, came the chanted words "To him that hath overcome is given a crown of life!" and again, "To him that hath endured to the end is given a white stone!" *

At length we reached the place where, in the gloom, still lay my sleeping body, couched upon a stone. But peering down upon them the stone was no longer a dark crude mass. It was

---

* The allusions are to James 1:12 and Revelation 2:17, respectively.—Ed.

a crystal cubical stone, upon the top of which rested three cornucopias, bearing corn, and wine, and oil; and against this, my stone of destiny, reposed my head, already faintly aureoled with light. My coronation was complete.

I knew that henceforth both my guide and my stone would be perfectly identified with me and that the contents of the cornucopias were the. emblems of my perpetual future nourishment and represented the harvest I had garnered in each of the three degrees I had just taken; Bread of Life from the first, Wine of Bliss and Illumination from the second, Oil of Wisdom from the third. Here was the realization of the familiar words, hitherto but fanciful poetic imagery: "Thou preparest a table before me in the presence of mine enemies; Thou anointest my head with oil; my cup runneth over!" (Psalm 23:5) Again my good Brother gripped me as a Master Mason. We drew together in an embrace of fellowship so fervent that we seemed to coalesce beyond the possibility of further separateness. "A measure of corn for a penny," he said to me, "and see thou hurt not the oil and the wine." (Revelation 6:6) And I understood his hint to be prudent in my use of them.

"*Ave, Frater, atque Vale!*" were his last spoken of words to me.[†]

And mine to him were "*Vale, Frater, atque Ave!*"

When I looked about me with the eyes of my flesh I was alone. Sunrise was breaking over the barren heath.

[†] "Hail, brother, and farewell!"

Chapter Four
The Past and Future of the Masonic Order

First, that which is natural;
after, that which is spiritual. —1 Corinthians 15:46

1. The Past

BEGINNINGS, whether of nations, religions, institutions, or even of the world and life itself, are notoriously obscure and difficult of precise fixation. The reason is that nothing actually "begins" to be, but there merely takes place a transformation into new conditions of something that preexisted in other conditions. Call the point or moment at which the change occurs a "beginning" if you wish; it will be found that such beginning is but an effect generated by, and issuing from, anterior causes. Life itself does not, at physical birth, begin to be; it merely then enters physical conditions and assumes physical guise. A corresponding change occurs at the birth or beginning of human institutions; they are developments and formalizations of something which previously existed in a fluid, incohesive condition. This is the case with Masonry, and accounts for the tradition that it is as old as man himself, whatever forms it has assumed, and that it is of divine origin.

Modern speculative Freemasonry had a beginning in the early years of the 18th century, but only in the sense that in 1717 originated that which afterwards developed into, and now subsists as, the English Masonic Constitution. Masonry itself existed long before that time, and in two forms: (1) exoterically, in the operative building guilds, and (2) esoterically, in a variety of secret communities of mystics and occultists, having no relation to the practical building trade but often using builders' terminology for symbolical purposes of their own.

Modern Masonry is a blend of both of these; its constitutions, charges, rituals, and instruction lectures incorporate elements drawn from each of them. The Ancient Charge, for instance, which is delivered to every Masonic candidate on admission to the Order today, is an example of what has come over from the operative Masons. It is patently an instruction of the kind one would expect to find given to a youth on becoming entered as an apprentice to a handicraft and embarking upon adult and civic responsibilities; it is a mere admonition to him to be a moral man, a worthy citizen, a creditable workman and member of his trade-guild, to fear God, honor the king, love his country, and generally educate and improve himself. It does not contain the least reference to any knowledge or wisdom of an extraordinary kind, or suggest any vestige of acquaintance with subjects of a mystical or occult character.

But on turning to the ceremonial rituals, especially that of the third degree, and to the "Traditional History" and instruction lectures, we find, mixed up with references to the operative Builders' trade, matters of a highly esoteric and mystical nature, having no possible operative or materialistic connection and not to be thought of as associated with the technical equipment of a workman in material stone and brick.

This esoteric element descended, of course, not from the operative guilds, but from less public organizations of symbolic or mystical Masons, and it is the latter alone whose necessarily obscure history and purpose repay investigation at this time of day.

These organizations were the representatives of a stream of Hermetic tradition and practice, the upper reaches of which go back into pre-Christian times, into Egypt, and to the Rabbinical mystics and Kabbalists, among whom existed a secret, guarded lore of the Cosmos and of human life; a lore which found only partial, though cryptic, expression in the Hebrew scriptures in terms of building. With them the building and the subsequent vicissitudes of Solomon's Temple (whether this was ever an historical material erection or not) provided a great glyph or mythos of the up-building of the human soul, whether considered individually or collectively; and as the course of Hebrew history advanced and the stream of circumstances and mystical tradition widened into its Christian development, the same symbolic terminology continued to be used.

Accordingly the Gospels, the Epistles, and the Apocalypse are found to teem with Masonic imagery and allusions to spiritual building. It is in these that the human soul becomes expressly declared to be the real Temple prefigured by the previous historic or quasi-historic one. A spiritual Chief Cornerstone, rejected by certain builders, is mentioned; one in which the entire social fabric is to grow together into a single universal Temple. St. John himself, as the "beloved disciple" or most advanced initiate of the Christian Master, becomes, according to the esoteric tradition, his Chief Warden and entrusted—as every Senior Warden in our symbolic lodges is—with the task of keeping order in the West and, after the days of his flesh, of occultly controlling from the heavens the development of the law of Christ in the Occidental world. Hence he became, and still is acknowledged as, the Masonic patron saint, and is found spoken of in the Rosicrucian reference in Dante's *Paradiso* as

> He that lay upon the breast
> Of Him who is our mystic pelican,
> And from the Cross was named for office blest [*]

... while one of his known pupils, St. Ignatius—who is reputed to have been the little child whom the Lord once took and set in the midst as a type of fitness for realizing the kingdom of heaven—is found expounding religion in these purely Masonic terms:

[*]   Dante, *The Divine Comedy: Paradiso*, canto 25, lines 112–114.

> Forasmuch as ye are stones of a Temple which were prepared
> beforehand for a building of God, the Father, being hoisted
> up to the heights by the working-tool of Jesus Christ, which
> is the Cross, and using for a rope the Holy Spirit; your faith
> being a windlass, and love the way leading up to God. So
> then ye are all Companions in the way, spiritual temples,
> carrying your Divine principle within you, your shrine,
> your Christ and your holy things, being arrayed from head
> to foot with the commandments of Christ. [†]

The pronounced Masonic imagery used by Ignatius (who
was martyred at Rome in A D 107) tends to corroborate the tradition that the Square, Level and Plumb-rule, now allocated
to the Master and two Wardens of a lodge, were originally associated with the bishop, priest and deacon, when serving at
the secret altars of the persecuted Christians. Put together,
the three tools form a cross, which, on the worshipers being
disturbed by the secular authorities, could quickly be knocked
apart and appear but as builders' implements.

The most popular religious book of the earliest Christian
centuries was *The Shepherd of Hermas*, a collection of teachings,
visions and similitudes, couched in terms of Masonic allegory
and veiling (as the title implied) the hermetic or esoteric instruction of some "Shepherd," as the hierophants and adept-
teachers of the mysteries were, and in the canonical Scriptures
are, uniformly designated.

To define the position which, after the event known as
the Christian Incarnation, seems to have been assumed by all
the mystical Builders, the spiritual Alchemists, the Rosicru-
cians, and the divers other schools of the secret gnosis who accepted that fact as the central pivotal one of human spiritual
evolution and the culmination of earlier mystery systems, it
may be said that they regarded themselves as one great Frater-

[†]   Ignatius, *Epistle to Ephesians*, chapter 9.

nity in the divine mysteries under the unseen but actual guidance of Jesus Christ, "the Carpenter" (Gr. *tekton*), as Supreme Grand Master, with the greater initiate, St. John the Divine, and the lesser initiate, St. John Baptist, as Senior and Junior Grand Wardens; the winter and summer solstices (the times of the sun's lowest annual declension and meridian height) being allocated to the two latter as festival days or time-points peculiarly favorable for spiritual contact between the Grand Lodge Above and the lesser lodges below.

All down the stream of history will be found the similitude of the human soul to a stone and directions for working it from a crude to a perfect state. The career of the patriarch Jacob begins with a stone. The Dervishes of the Arabian Desert are given a cubed stone smeared with blood on their initiation. The sacred object and palladium of the Muslim faith is the Kaaba or Cubical Stone. The stone is found described as *lapis exilis* and *lapis ex coelis*; it is always one said to have come from heaven, whence it is now in exile in this outer world. As a protest against materializing the idea of it, one finds exclamations such as Cornelius Agrippa's famous *Transmutemini! Transmutemini in viventes lapides!*—"become ye transformed into living stones!"* Those more advanced mystics, the spiritual alchemists, have provided us with a wealth of obscure lore concerning the "Stone of the Philosophers"; and all through the Christian centuries, behind the activities of public elementary religion and the official work of the Church, can be traced evidences of this higher, esoteric, more abstruse and difficult

* The original alchemical saying is *Transmutemini... Transmutemini de lapidimus mortuis in vivos lapides philosophicos,* "Transform, transform yourself from dead stones into living philospher's stones," and first appeared in the *Clavis Totius Philosophiae Chymisticae* by Gerard Dorn (1530–1584). The ultimate origin of the saying is biblical: "Let yourselves be built like living stones into a spiritual house, a holy priesthood..." (1 Peter 2:5) This is paralleled in the monitorial instruction of the Entered Apprentice degree: "Thereby fitting our minds as living stones for that spiritual building, that house not made with hands, eternal in the heavens."—Ed.

work of mystical masonry and stone-working being wrought by abbots, monks, and laymen, either in solitude or communities of less or greater size, yet in severest concealment.

The history of this movement in England cannot be written in detail here, but a few points of it may be cited as evidence of the fact that, beyond all operative-trade connections, the primary work of masonry was one of mystical religion and had to do with the arcana of the human soul; that it was an intellectual and a spiritual science promoting the development of the individual initiate and, through him, the advancement of the general weal.

The English Masonic Constitutions of 1784, for example, reproduce a memorandum "concernynge the Mystery of Maconrye," said to have been written early in the 15th century by King Henry VI with his own hand—probably for private rather than for state purposes, since he himself is alleged to have been made a Mason. † Transposing his words from archaic into modern English, the King's memorandum indicates as follows: that Masonry is a spiritual science; that it originated in the East (in both a mystical and a geographical sense) and reached the junior human races in the West through traveling Phoenicians (misdescribed as "Venetians"); that its development had been greatly advanced by Pythagoras (curiously miscalled by the English names "Peter Gower"), who, after receiving his own initiations, founded the great Crotona school and instructed others in the science; that the science itself involves knowledge of and power over hidden forces of nature, so that the expert Mason can perform acts which to the uninitiated would appear miraculous; that progress in the science comes by instruction, practice and silence; that the science is to be imparted only to worthy and suitable men, since abuse of it and of the powers arising with it would result in both personal

† This document is known to Masonic historians as the Leland Manuscript, and can be found in many classic reference works on the subject of the Old Charges.—Ed.

and general evil; that Masons understand and can effect the art of alchemical transmutation and possess a universal symbolic language of their own by which they can intercommunicate, whatever their race or country; that they have the "skill of becoming good and perfect," apart from all motives of fear and hope such as influence lesser minds and are held out by popular religion; that not all Masons realize their attainments or become perfect, for many fail in capacity, and more still in the arduous personal effort essential to the acquisition of this wisdom.

The genuineness of the King's memorandum has been questioned, though *prima facie* it is well attested. But whether a genuine script of his or not, its contents, within their limits, accurately represent the nature of Masonry itself.

No one can read English or European history from the period of that memorandum onward without realizing that to that history there has been an inner side not cognized or treated of by academic historians, or without feeling behind the march of external events—and as it were connected with or even directing them—the concealed presence of minds more than normally capable: initiates, possessing and wielding the very powers testified to in Henry VI's memorandum. The lives and literary remains of such men as—to name no others—Paracelsus, Abbot Tritheim, Basil Valentine, Jacob Boehme, George Johan Gichtel, Thomas Vaughan, and Elias Ashmole, provide above-surface indications of a strong current of sub-surface activity, a current of which no record exists or is ever likely now to be made. But to that current one must look for the perpetuation of the secret Masonic science, and to its projection, in a highly diluted and elementary form, into publicity in modern speculative Masonry.

The religious Reformation of the 15th century was the first great episode in a far-reaching revolutionary movement in the intellectual, social and political life of the West, a movement the end of which is not yet. Amid the intensifying unspirituality and materialism of the times and the impending disintegration of public instituted religion, a decision seems to have been come to by some far-seeing enlightened minds to put forward the old mystical gnosis and tradition in a simple form and to attempt to interest a small section of the public in it. This suggestion is incapable of rigorous proof, and will perhaps commend itself only to those who are in any measure conscious of the inner mechanism controlling the visible clock-face of historic events. But be this as it may, we find, about the year 1600 and onwards, the first small signs of a movement that has eventuated in the vast modern Masonic Craft, with its as yet further indeterminate possibilities.

The first recorded reception of a non-operative Mason to an operative lodge occurred at Edinburgh in 1600. The operative lodges were then becoming obsolete and defunct, and by 1620 operative Masonry had become entirely superseded in London by speculative, the members of the former working no longer in guilds but striving still to keep alive their old form of fellowship. The first traceable initiation, on English soil, of a non-operative Mason occurred at Newcastle in 1641; and the second—that of Elias Ashmole, already a student of arcane science—at Warrington in 1646. Accretions to the ranks of the Craft proceeded to be made, but were at first few and gradual, owing to disturbed political conditions. The Charter of the Royal Society, dated 1663, as drawn up by Dr. (afterwards Sir) Christopher Wren, seems to have been prepared with a view to giving official sanction not to science as at present secularly understood and pursued, but to science of a more occult character such as Masonry as before defined deals with, for the preamble of that document refers to private meetings of certain men devoted to the investigation of the "hidden causes of things" in the public interest. *

* Wilmshurst refers here to the Royal Society. From an unofficial "Invisible College" that began meeting in the 1640s to study of ideas of Francis Bacon, the Royal Society eventually evolved into one of the leading institutions for the advancement of scientific knowledge. One

In 1717 four old London lodges combined to constitute a new nucleus. From them the first Grand Lodge was formed and thus modern Masonry was born, at an inn, the Apple Tree Tavern, in Lincoln's Inn Fields.

In 1721 Dr. Anderson was entrusted with the drawing up of the Constitutions of the new community. The conditions of the Craft in that year may be deduced from a statement of the eminent antiquary Dr. Stukeley, who writes:

> I was the first person made a free mason in London for many years. We had great difficulty to find members enough to perform the ceremony. Immediately after that it took a run, & ran itself out of breath thru' the folly of its members. *

of Bacon's expressions, "the hidden causes of things," was invoked in the 28 November, 1660 address that Sir Christopher Wren gave at the inaugural meeting of the Society—a reading of the draft charter which they intended the King of England to approve: "And whereas we are well informed that a competent number of persons of eminent learning, ingenuity, and honour, concording in their inclinations and studies toward this employment, have for some time accustomed themselves to meet weekly, and orderly to confer about the hidden causes of things, with a design to establish certain and correct theories in philosophy; and by their labours in the disquisition of nature to prove themselves real benefactors to mankind; and that they have already made a considerable progress by [many] useful and remarkable discoveries, inventions, and experiments in the improvement of mathematics, mechanics, astronomy, navigation, physic[s], and chemistry, we have determined to grant our royal favour, patronage and all due encouragement to this illustrious assembly, and so beneficial and laudable an enterprise." [Cited from Allan Cunningham, *The Lives of the Most Eminent British Painters, Sculptors and Architects* (London: John Murray, 1831), vol. 4, pp. 165–166.] A number of those present were Freemasons, including Sir Wren himself, and Sir Robert Moray, who may have been one of the creators of the Masonic rituals [see David Stevenson, *The Origins of Freemasonry: Scotland's Century* (Cambridge University Press, 1988)].—Ed.

* *The Family Memoirs of the Rev. William Stukeley*, M. D. (Durham: Andrews & Co., 1882), p. 122.

Abuses supervened from the admission of all and sundry without due qualifications. In 1724 a Brother protested in a public journal that

> 'Tis my opinion that the late Prostitution of our Order is in some Measure the betraying it. The weak heads of Vintners, Drawers, Wigmakers, Weavers, etc., admitted into our Fraternity, have not only brought contempt upon the Institution, but do very much endanger it. [†]

In the same year was established "for poor brethren" the first benevolent fund, which since has developed into the great Charity organizations now connected with the Craft.

In the course of the next fifty years the numbers of the Craft so increased that central headquarters were found advisable, and on May Day of 1775, the foundation-stone of the present Freemasons' Hall in London was laid with great ceremony.

Despite the fact that men were being admitted to the Order who were little qualified to appreciate the science of Masonry, and that consequently the understanding of that science was becoming increasingly debased, elements of the original intention still remained, and echoes of it can be caught in some of the recorded incidents of the occasion.

In the foundation-stone itself was inserted a plate perpetuating the event and the names of the then Grand Master, his deputy and the Grand Wardens; and stating that Masonry was of heavenly origin, "*descendit e coelo*"; and concluding with the maxim of Solon in Greek characters, "Know thyself."[‡]

At the religious service performed upon the occasion was sung an anthem of praise to the Great Architect:

[†]   *The Plain-Dealer*, September 14, 1724. Cited in Robert Freke Gould, *The Concise History of Freemasonry* (1903), p. 209.—Ed.

[‡]   ΓΝΩΘΙ ΣΕΑΥΤΟΝ —Ed.

Who deign'd the human soul to raise
By mystic secrets sprung from heaven. *

...while a specially composed ode affirmed of the new *Aula Latomorum* that:

...religion, untainted, here dwells;
Here the morals of Athens are taught;
Great Hiram's tradition here tells
How the world out of chaos was brought. †

From these extracts it is clear that, at least to its leading minds, Masonry was a secret science of soul-building, and that the great central legend and mythos expressed in the traditional history in the Craft's third degree referred to no events in earthly time or history, but to Cosmic events of a metaphysical and mystical character. Further, from the preface to the *Constitutions* of 1784 it is made clear that the practical builder's art is to be considered only as the substratum of speculative Masonry; that the history of the operative side is negligible, for when speculative Masons became a separate body of men the science had no further concern with practical building; and that the speculative work is a personal mystical one, rising like a pyramid "tending regularly up to a summit of attainments, ever concealed by intervening clouds from the promiscuous multitudes of common observers below."

---

*   Dedication anthem by Henry Dagge, published in the special 1776 supplement to the 1767 edition of Anderson's *Constitutions* (p. lxxi). Dagge borrowed his wording from James Eyre Weeks' *Solomon's Temple: An Oratorio*, which was published in the Antients' *Ahiman Rezon* in 1756. This interesting poetical work is reprinted in full in Shawn Eyer (Ed.), *Our Wine Has a Spring: Four Centuries of Masonic Poetry* (San Francisco: Plumbstone, 2008).—Ed.

†   The entire ode was printed in William Preston, *Illustrations of Masonry* (1792 edition), pp. 373–374.—Ed.

Freemasons' Hall being completed, it was, on 23rd May 1776, triply dedicated, again with great ceremony; firstly to Masonry; a second time to Virtue; and a third time to Universal Charity and Benevolence. The last-named of the three purposes came in course of time to dominate completely at least the first of them. The Craft became a great money-raising institution for relieving its own needy members and their relatives, and as a charitable society does excellent work which commands the devoted interest of many good brethren who know nothing, and seek to know nothing, of Masonry itself in its only proper and primary aspect of spiritual science, and who regard it merely as a luxurious item of social life and maintain their connection with it solely from philanthropic motives.

From the facts thus roughly outlined it is clear that the pre-1717 brethren were men of a very different caliber, and held a vastly higher conception of Masonry, from those who subsequently came to constitute the Craft and have expanded it to its present great dimensions. Of the latter class, whatever their merits, virtues, and good works in other respects, they cannot be said to have been either theoretic or practical mystics or to have cultivated the knowledge of Masonry as that science must be primarily understood. They cannot say of themselves as their predecessors truly could and did:

We have the Mason Word and second sight[‡]

... for growth in the life of the spirit and the enhanced faculty and inward vision that come therewith have not been within the ambit of their desire.

As one of the most deeply learned and understanding writers upon the subject (the authoress of *A Suggestive Inquiry into the Hermetic Mystery*) affirms:

‡   From "The Muses' Threnodie" (circa 1630) by Henry Adamson, line 911.

The outward form (or present practice) of Masonry is too
absurd to be perpetuated were it not for a certain secret response of common sense to the original mystery. The initiated moved one another on by words of power. The Masons
ape this but have lost the magic key to open the door into
the Hermetic garden. They want the words, which are only
to be found by seeking them in the subjective fundamental life, from which they are as far out as the tools they use.
The true tools also may be found on the way in; they will be
given one after another as they are wanted. [*]

Another learned author, who had every motive to speak
well of the Craft—the late Brother John Yarker—was constrained to write in 1872, in his able and most instructive *Notes
on the Scientific and Religious Mysteries* that:

> As the Masonic fraternity is now governed, the Craft is fast
> becoming the paradise of the bon vivant, of the "charitable"
> hypocrite who forgets the version of St. Paul and adorns his
> breast with the "charity jewel"; (having by this judicious
> expenditure obtained the "purple," he metes out judgment
> to other brethren of greater ability and morality but less
> means); the manufacturer of paltry masonic tinsel. . . . No
> other institution is so intrinsically valuable as Craft Ma-
> sonry, or capable of such superhuman things. As now gov-
> erned, few societies perform less. None profess such great
> objects; few accomplish so very little real and substantial
> good. May reformation be speedy and effective. [†]

Such facts are not pleasant to contemplate, nor would
they be proclaimed here without good purpose and a constructive motive. But it is well to face them before proceeding

[*]   Wilmshurst's adaptation of M. A. Atwood's *A Suggestive Inquiry into the
      Hermetic Mystery*, pp. 578–579.—Ed.
[†]   John Yarker, *Notes on the Scientific and Religious Mysteries*, pp. 157–158.

further, since what remains to be said will not only deal with a happier aspect of the subject, but is based upon the premise that the otherwise deplorable perversion and materialization of the true Masonic intention has been both an inevitable and a necessary prelude to a spiritual efflorescence which in due course will manifest itself and of which the beginnings are already perceptible.

In no censorious or reproachful spirit, therefore, are such observations as the foregoing recorded. They might indeed be extensively amplified if to do so would serve any useful purpose, but no one with intimate experience of the Craft will fail to recognize either their truth or the cogency of their reproach. It is undeniable that, through ignorance of the true principles of Masonry, the Craft has suffered itself to become debased and overrun with members lacking alike the intellectuality, the temperament, and the desire, to appreciate those principles. today's newspaper, for example, contains the advertisement of a turf bookmaker who proclaims himself to be "on the square," and on the strength of that qualification seeks to engage the services of a betting-tout. It is well known that commercial houses today find it advantageous, for business purposes, to insist upon their more important employees being members of the Order. In the Order itself advancement is notoriously connected with social position and the extent of a member's contributions to the charities. honors, and even medals, are bestowed for money payments to this or that subscription list. Any man with a title, from a mayor to a prince, needs only to be a Mason a matter of months to find himself elevated to some figurehead position in the Craft, without the least merit of a purely Masonic kind or any understanding of the science itself. The central ideas and teachings of the Craft are left unexplained; ceremonies are discharged quite perfunctorily, and with the majority are of entirely subservient importance to the indissociable feasting and wearisome rounds of speech-making that follow; and the general ignorance of

Masonic truth provides ample scope for the self-assertion of men whose ideas of moral grandeur and Masonic virtue are evidenced by an ambition to attain office in the Craft and to adorn their persons with as much purple and jewelery as they can acquire.

It is all woefully wrong and misconceived. Of course worthier *traits* exist. The heart of English Masonry is sound, if its head be obtuse and muddled, and the work of its hands not of the character it might and ought to be.

When the worst has been said that can be charged against the methods of modern Masonry, it amounts merely to an exhibition of venial human weakness, vanity and sycophancy, the growth of which, while obscuring and falsifying Masonic principles, has been due to failure to grasp what those principles imply and entail. Many tares have sprung up among the corn; but good corn has not failed to grow, and that the two can grow together in the same field is a tribute to the richness of the soil from which both spring and the nourishing power of the Masonic intention, which, like sunlight, shines impartially upon both and quickens whatever seed is sown within its field, whether tares or wheat.

There are few received into the Craft to whom Masonry does not bring, if but dimly and momentarily, some measure of new vision, some impulse towards its ideals; few who do not feel it to contain something far greater than they know or than appears upon its surface presentation. Moreover, in the deep heart of every man exists a responsiveness to ultimate truth, and a fondness, amounting sometimes to a passion, for it when expressed in ceremonial grandeur and impressiveness—a subconscious reminiscence, as Plato would explain—of truth and glories it has once known and must one day know again, and which Masonic ritual does something to revive, as was of course the intention of all the initiation systems of the past and is still the intention of our present Order. And how often one finds minds which are denied, or which would repudiate, the use of symbolic ritual in their church, leap to it with admiration and affection in their lodge, as though the Protestant rejection, in the religious sphere, of the rich symbolism and sacramentalism wisely once devised for instructing eye, ear, and mind, and exalting the imagination towards spiritual verities, had starved them of their rightful nourishment. It is not surprising that to many such minds Masonry becomes, as they themselves say, a religion, or at all events a precious fact to which their souls respond however inarticulately, and that for them the door of the lodge is, as was once said of the altar-rails, "the thin barrier dividing the world of sense from the world of spirit."

2. The Future

In the fact that, amidst so much imperfect apprehension of its meaning and intention, Masonry should not only have survived, but should continue to make an ever-widening appeal to the imagination, exists the proof that, inherent in it, however deeply veiled, is a vibrant, indestructible vital principle which awakens a never-failing response, whether loud or feeble, in its devotees. The Light is in the darkness, though as yet that darkness comprehendeth it not. The modern Craftsman may not as yet "have the Mason Word" in his own possession, like his earlier brethren; but, nevertheless, that Word itself abides within the Masonic system, and he faintly hears and responds to its overtones; it is, for most, a Lost Word, but it patiently awaits recovery; and many today are impatiently seeking to find it.

That vital principle became implanted in the Order system by those wise, far-seeing, now untraceable minds which, as we have said, some three centuries ago conceived and inspired, if they did not directly devise, the formation of the Order as a means of perpetuating in an elementary way the ancient secret doctrine through a period of darkness and disruption, and until such time as that doctrine, and the mysteries that once taught it, can again be revived in a larger way.

The evidences of the presence in the Masonic system and texts of the ancient arcane teaching, are threefold. Firstly, the grading of the system itself into the three traditional stages of spiritual perfecting, involving in turn the discipline and purification of the body and sense-nature; the control, self-knowledge and illumination of the mind; and, finally, that entire abnegation of the will and death of the sense of personality which lead to union with the divine will, beyond personality and separateness. Secondly, the incorporation of the myths of the building of Solomon's Temple and the death of Hiram, both of which are allegories and portray not historic, but metaphysical, truth of profound importance. Thirdly, the insertion into the texts of the ceremonies and side-lectures of a number of pieces of esoteric teaching common to all the initiation-doctrine of East and West, but not known to be such by the average Brother who is unfamiliar with that doctrine, and so cryptically expressed and so interwoven with more elementary moral teaching as only to be recognizable to the more fully instructed observer. Examples of this esoteric teaching and of its implications are given in the second section of this volume, dealing with "Light on the Way."

The compilation of the text of the present rituals and instruction lectures is supposed to have been, and no doubt was, undertaken in or soon after 1717, by Dr. Anderson and others whose personality is now of no moment.* Nor is it material to inquire how far those compilers were deliberately obscuring and crypticizing occult knowledge they personally possessed or, if personally lacking it, were unconsciously led into per-

---

*   Royal Arch Masonry was introduced into England in 1778 by a Jewish Brother, Moses Michael Hayes. [Here the author is incorrect. Moses Michael Hayes (1739–1805) was an American of Dutch Jewish descent. He become an avid Freemason and helped spread Masonry throughout New England. He was Master of lodges in New York, Rhode Island and Massachusetts, and served as Grand Master of the Massachusetts Grand Lodge (Scottish constitution) from 1788 to 1792. Records of Royal Arch workings in England date back to at least 1752, when Brother Hayes was but 13 years of age.—Ed.]

petuating greater wisdom than they knew. The subject has been ably and exhaustively discussed in a work of very high value to the Masonic student, *Studies in Mysticism* by Brother A. E. Waite, who takes the view that the compilers did not for the most part know what they were doing, yet that they wrote as if guided by a blind though unerring instinct "which made even the foolish old scholars of the past see through their inverted and scoriated glasses something of what Masonry actually is, and therefore, in the midst of much idle talk, they provided, unconsciously to themselves, a Master Key of the Sanctuary."[†]

This is probably a true verdict, for from various evidences Anderson and his colleagues show little signs of having been esotericists of any depth or ability. But, be it accurate or not, the fact remains that our system was so designed and devised as to be a true compendium of universal initiation; one that reproduces the salient features of every system that has existed, or that elsewhere still exists, for advancing human perfecting.

In that fact lies the strength, the vitality, the attractive power, of the Masonic system; the subtle charm that it casts over minds sensitive to its implications, but as yet unable to interpret them or to understand their own responsiveness to them. And in the demonstration and elucidation of the doctrine concealed in the system lies the hope of the Craft gradually educating itself and fulfilling its original design in the years now before it.

The point up to which these observations are meant to lead can now be stated. It is that before the true spirit and inward content of Masonry could be appreciated upon a scale sufficiently wide to constitute the Order a real spiritual force in the social body (as one hopes and sees indications that it will become), it has been necessary in the first instance to build up a great, vigorous and elaborate physical organization as a vehi-

† A. E. Waite, *Studies in Mysticism and Certain Aspects of the Secret Tradition* (1908), p. 291.

cle in which that spirit may eventually and efficaciously manifest. In view of the importance of the ultimate objective aimed at, it matters nothing that from two to three centuries have been needed to develop that organization, to build up that requisite physical framework, or that the material of which it has been constructed has not been so far of ideal quality. With the larger prospect in view we can afford to look both charitably and philosophically upon momentary matters that may be regarded as regrettable and as falling far below the standard of even the surface and letter of Masonic principle; we can be content that the Order has been composed so largely of men little understanding or capable of assimilating its profounder purpose; that its energies have run off from their true channel to the subsidiary ones of social amenities and charitable relief; that its higher ranks have been filled, not with adepts and experts in spiritual science, capable of ministering wisdom and instruction to the humbler ranks below (as the symbolism of our great hierarchical system surely implies their doing), but with "great kings, dukes and lords" and other social dignitaries, displaying no signs of possessing arcane wisdom and placed in their complimentary or administrative positions (which they nevertheless admirably and efficiently fulfill) merely to give the Order social sanction and—as the nauseous doggerel runs—"our myst'ries to put a good grace on." *

The growth of a great institution—a nation, a Church, a system of the mysteries—is a slow growth, proceeding from material apparently unpromising, and involving continual selection, rejection, and refining, before something becomes finally sublimated from it and forged into an efficient instrument. To take the most appropriate analogy, the erection of Solomon's Temple was a work of years, of diversely collected material and engaging numerous interests; but not until it was completed, dedicated and consecrated as a tabernacle

* From "The Entered 'Prentices Song" by Matthew Birkhead, published in the first edition of Anderson's *Constituions* (1723), p. 84.—Ed.

worthy of the *Shekhinah*, did that Presence descend upon it, illumining and flooding, the whole House and enabling the earthy vehicle to fulfill a spiritual purpose.

So now, too, with the Masonic Order. As a physical vehicle, a material organization, it is as complete, as elaborated and as efficiently controlled, as perhaps it can ever be expected to be. It now stands awaiting illumination. That illumination must come from within itself, as the Divine Presence manifested within the symbolic Temple. The Order awaits the liberation and realization of its own inner consciousness, hitherto dormant and repressed by surface-elements now proving to be of no, or of illusory, value. No sooner is the deeper and true nature of the Masonic design revealed to brethren than upon all hands they leap to recognition of it and desire to realize it; and, for such, there can be no going back to old ways and old outlooks. The people that have sat in darkness have seen glimpses of a great light; they will now cultivate that light themselves, and be the means that others behold it also. In this way the Craft throughout the world will become gradually regenerated in its understanding and so fulfill the destiny planned for it by those who inspired its formation three centuries ago. And it will become in due course the portal to still higher and more important spiritual events.

The coming change must be and will be worked out, not from anything emanating from the higher ranks of the Craft— the Grand Lodge and Provincial Grand Lodges—but from the floor of the individual private lodge. For the private lodge is the Masonic unit. The higher ranks are but recruited therefrom at present for complimentary or administrative purposes, although when the time comes for those hierarchies to realize their own symbolic value, it will be their members who will descend upon the lodges of common Craftsmen, no longer as makers of merely complimentary speeches, but as real authorities upon Masonic wisdom and instructive missionaries and purveyors of Masonic truth. The private lodge is the point from which the transformation must be achieved. One such lodge in a town or district, that applies itself to Masonic work upon the lines indicated in these pages, will be as a powerful leavening influence and set up wholesome reactions in neighboring lodges. Some resistance, and even derision, may be anticipated at first from those content with old standards and not yet ripe to appreciate a higher one, for the "nations" of less refined understanding may always be expected to "rage furiously together" at any suggestion involving departure from habitual methods or implying a possible reflection upon their wisdom. This, however, can be met with patience and charitable thought, and will soon disappear before a quiet, resolute adherence to principle. Moreover, the problem of the admission of unsuitable applicants for membership of a lodge will soon settle itself when the standard of Masonic interpretation has been thus raised.

Let it here be emphasized that nothing in this volume is intended to advocate the least departure from or alteration of current Masonic working, or any deflection from loyalty to established usage or the governing authority. Those forms are so efficiently contrived, so perfectly adapted to the work of the Order, that, save perhaps in a matter of detail here and there, they can be altered only to their disadvantage and at the peril of disturbing ancient landmarks fixed where they are with greater wisdom than is perhaps at present recognized. Even as things are, in the haste to get through ceremonial work as quickly as may be, there is an unfortunate tendency already in official quarters to clip and curtail certain ceremonies, thereby depriving the brethren of some valuable and significant pieces of ritual which, if continued to remain unworked, will soon become obsolete and forgotten.

Nevertheless, a little flexibility in matters of lodge procedure would be permissible and is even desirable when degrees are conferred. Merely to reel off a memorized ritual in a formal, mechanical way too often results in but mechanical effects, and the subject of the ceremony goes away perhaps unimpressed or bewildered. There is nothing to prevent the delivery of the official rite being supplemented by unofficial words of explanation and encouragement such as would lend that rite additional impressiveness, a more intimate and personal bearing, and awaken in him who undergoes it a more deep and real sense of becoming vitally incorporated into living truth and into a Brotherhood to whom that truth is no mere sentiment but a profound reality. Moreover, with a view to inducing favorable atmosphere and conditions for the conferment of a ceremony, before the candidate enters, the assembled brethren should always be notified from the Chair that they are about to engage in a deeply solemn act which claims the concentrated thought and aspiration of each of them, to the intent that what is done and signified ceremonially may be realized spiritually in both themselves and him to whom they desire to minister. Further, the ceremonial preparation of the candidate before being brought into the lodge should be treated, not with levity or as a mere incidental formality, but as a profoundly sacramental act, in the significance of which both the officiating deacons and the candidate himself should be instructed. Let all brethren be assured that there is no detail of Masonic ceremonial but is charged with very deep purpose and significance; this will appear to them more and more fully and luminously in proportion to their faithful endeavor to realize the intention of even simple and apparently unimportant points of ritual.

Sundry other matters may here be mentioned as deserving the consideration of the Craft.

The first is the coordination of the rituals with a view to securing uniformity of working and instruction throughout the Craft, coupled with a certain but slight amount of desirable revision. An official standardized ritual would be beneficial and would no doubt be widely adopted even if its adoption were left optional to lodges preferring to continue their

present form of working.* Upon all new lodges, constituted
after the date of standardization, the official working should
be imposed, so that, in course of time, virtual uniformity of
procedure would be achieved.

The present divergences in the working of lodges are not
great and are easily capable of adjustment so as to secure a
common footing of work throughout the Craft. Some lodges
use points of working not used in others and which they are
rightly jealous in desiring to conserve; for example, many
lodges neither work nor know of the traditional five signs connected with the third. degree, and merely communicate three
of them, omitting two which are of great significance. On the
other hand, some lodges retain details brought over from the
operative bodies, details now obsolete and without moment
to speculative Masonry and which nowadays might well be
dropped. The "Ancient Charge" delivered to Entered Apprentices on their reception is an instance of an operative tradition,
for which, if it be not abandoned altogether, an alternative
Charge, more suited to present conditions and more in con-
sonance with speculative Masonry, might well be substituted.
For a Charge that was intended for, and that was delivered
to, youths upon entering an operative building guild is un-
suited to men already immersed in civic, family, and business
responsibilities, and seeking now to acquire knowledge of a
purely mystical character; it is absurd and grotesque. to counsel a middle-aged experienced man to perform elementary duties of citizenship, or to express to—perhaps an ecclesiastical
dignitary who joins the Order, the hope that he "will become
respectable in life!"†

---

* With few exceptions, American Masonic jurisdictions require a uniform
   ceremony in all their lodges. But elsewhere, as Wilmshurst describes,
   it is not uncommon for ritual to vary from lodge to lodge.—Ed.

† This is not a feature of the first degree charges in use in the United
   States. The English version, which still includes the verbiage
   against which Wilmshurst protests, says: "And as a last and general
   recommendation, let me exhort you to dedicate yourself to such

Revision of the rituals would, of course, be a delicate task; one not to be undertaken at haphazard or to meet the chance whims and uninstructed notions of this or that brother, but one calling for the enlightened guidance of minds conversant with initiation science; otherwise the Craft may lose more than it may gain, and good plants may be pulled up and thrown away in mistake for weeds. As an example of a point needing revision and excision, let me instance those passages in which a candidate is enjoined to extend charity and relief to those needing it "if he can do so without detriment to himself or connections." These qualifying words surely vitiate the whole spirit of "charity." If charity means anything—and mere financial help is not charity, but only one form of its practical manifestation—it involves a wise but unstinted selflessness, a self-sacrifice at whatever personal cost. To hedge round that supreme virtue with a cautious verbal reservation in one's own favor is a limitation entirely unworthy of Masonic magnanimity and the words come as a shock to one's moral sensitiveness.

To come to the next point: the Festive Board. In previous pages it has been indicated that the customary practice of refreshment and social conviviality is not only practically useful, but has a deep sacramental value. It is, of course, technically extra-Masonic and non-official, or perhaps quasi-official; but it provides real and useful opportunities for fraternizing, and intellectual opportunities for enlarging upon Masonic matters not dealt with in the lodge sanctuary itself; while, in its symbolic and higher aspect, it illustrates that relaxation from labor, and that refreshment derived from the inter-communion of those united in a common work, which in the providential order are arranged for us both in this life and hereafter.

The value, or otherwise, of the Festive Board, depends, therefore, upon its good use or its abuse. If it be regarded and

pursuits as may render you respectable in life, useful to mankind, and an ornament to the society of which you have this day become a member." Cited from *The Complete Workings of Craft Freemasonry* (London: Lewis Masonic, 1982), p. 62.—Ed.

used as the natural extension of the more formal work of the lodge, it can exercise a ministry of great service; if, on the other hand, it be but an occasion for junketing and social frivolity under the cover of Masonry, but with little or no Masonic relevance, it is apt to become a thing of reproach; the sublimities of the lodge-work are falsified by it and any good issuing from that work is forthwith neutralized. The test of true Masonic devotion and sincerity would be the honest answer each Brother can give to the question: "How far would my interest in Masonry extend and continue, if the practice of the Festive Board did not exist and Masonic proceedings were confined to the formal work of the lodge?" With this reflection the matter may be left to the good judgment of the Craft.

There must also be mentioned a question which has already rankled as a thorn in the side of Grand Lodge and will doubtless become still more troublesome—the "women's question"—and if I approach it, it is not with the idea of presuming to offer suggestions to the governing authority of the Craft, but of defining the position for the guidance of the average brother.

As things stand, Grand Lodge is the trustee of a system which it has inherited, which it is pledged to continue upon established lines, and which it has no power to alter if it wished, save at the request and by the common consent of those whose interests it exists to conserve. It has no power to sanction the admission of women into the order, nor is there any desire in its ranks that it should; indeed the fact that women can today take elsewhere precisely the same degrees as the Craft confers is a fact unknown to the majority of brethren.

Whether Grand Lodge should extend official recognition to societies professing to be Masonic and admitting members of both sexes is another matter, and depends upon the view to be taken of the regularity or irregularity of the societies in question. Can such societies produce satisfactory evidence of their regularity and right to recognition, or have they sprung into existence through the treachery or disloyalty of members of the Craft? That is not a question falling to the present writer to determine, nor has he sufficient material before him to do so. The only conclusion he can come to for himself, and the only advice he can offer to others, is to abide loyally by the existing ordinances of the duly constituted authority. The Craft so far has been the "Men's House," and must so remain until such time as circumstances—which do not now exist and for a long time to come are unlikely to exist—clearly warrant a departure from the present position. It may be that the "men" do not make the best use of their "house"; it may be that the now banned societies have sprung into existence because of that fact; it may be—and there are grounds for supposing it—that in those societies Masonry is worked with greater decorum, a far fuller understanding, a deeper reverence and appreciation of what it implies, than in the orthodox Craft.* But the fact remains that we are committed and pledged to our own Constitution for the present and we shall do neither it nor our individual selves a service by departing from strict loyalty to it.

Upon the general question of the fitness of women to receive the Masonic or any alternative form of initiation, I must record an affirmative conviction of the same strength as the negative one I make to the suggestion that women should be admitted to the Craft or that visiting relations between the latter and the unauthorized societies should be sanctioned; for, in existing conditions, such relationship is undesirable and might prove disastrous to both. Although the sexes meet upon a common footing in the field of both religious and secular affairs, and although the whole modern tendency is towards equality of rights, function and responsibility, Masonry at present stands outside both the religious and the secular categories, and by the majority of its members is viewed merely

* Taking into consideration Wilmshurst's interest in theosophy, he is likely referring to the theosophically-inclined co-masonic lodges which were not uncommon in England at the time he was writing.—Ed.

as a social luxury and a casual appendage to other activities of life. Until it is accorded a far higher appreciation than this, until it can be viewed from a standpoint not merely of ordinary morality but from one involving a high standard of personal sanctity; until the mental conception of it is sufficiently lofty and compelling to neutralize emotional frailty and the chances of moral lapse, Masonry is far better reserved as the "Men's House," even though that house be, in the prophet's words, one "of untempered mortar" and lacking the advantage of feminine association.

The human soul is essentially sexless, yet to the feminine side of humanity is notoriously credited exceptional intuitive power and capacity for the finer apprehension of truth, and upon this account, in the days of the Eleusinia, women were never excluded from initiation into the mysteries, but were allotted special rites of their own, and, in the processions of the Thesmophoria, passed along the public street bearing upon their heads the volumes of the sacred law: an eloquent symbolic tribute and testimony to the superior power of the feminine understanding to intuit the finer sense and implications of that Law.* It was to a woman—the mysterious Diotima of Megara—that the amazed Socrates owed his supreme initiation into that last Mystery of Love about which he speaks in the *Symposium* with such awe and moving eloquence; yet a woman with whom stands exhibited, in purposed contrast, that opposite pole of womanhood—the futile, mindless Xantippe whom he had wedded. There have been Egerias, Aspasias and Hypatias, besides those known to history; and Dante's hierophantess, Beatrice—all but archetypes of that "eternal womanly" which, Goethe truly divined†, always exists with us to lead

---

* It is important to bear in mind that the classical Greeks did not have anything like a Bible. Although the scholia (commentaries of later Christian scribes) on Theocritus did record that the women at the Thesmophoria carried "books of law" on their heads, this testimony is now viewed with skepticism by modern scholars.—Ed.

† Goethe's *Faust* concludes with the words *Das Ewig-Weibliche Zieht uns hinan.*—"The eternal feminine draws us upward."—Ed.

the male intellect ever upward and on. It is almost needless to point to the mass of work done by women still living in the exposition of mystical philosophy and religion, or to say that such great mines of instruction in matters of Masonic moment as *Isis Unveiled*, *The Secret Doctrine*, and *A Suggestive Inquiry into the Hermetic Mystery*, have come from the pens of women learned and enlightened in things pertaining to the Craft to a degree seldom evidenced by its own members.

In every interest, then, it is desirable that the "women's question" should rest where it is. Nothing can prevent those, of whichever sex, who are really builders in the spirit, from privately fraternizing in that spirit. To such, formal collaboration, however agreeable it might be were it permissible, can be dispensed with, for their work is not dependent upon facilities of a formal character, and they will be the first to recognize the wisdom of Order accepting and the expedience of conforming to current technical necessity. When the time and conditions arrive for present barriers to be removed, it will be because the Craft itself will have removed them by entering into a fuller realization of its purpose than now obtains, and because Grand Lodge will have been influenced to alter its laws by an authority higher even than itself—the Grand Lodge Above.

To pass now from these considerations of things of the moment to the larger vista towards which those things are leading, what is the prospect before the Order?

That prospect is perhaps sufficiently indicated by the familiar words written at the head of this paper: "First, that which is natural; after, that which is spiritual." (1 Corinthians 15:46) For nearly three centuries the Craft has been developing from a small germ to a great robust body characterized by tendencies of a purely natural kind, manifesting natural human weaknesses, and displaying the inexperience, the irresponsibility, and the limitations of outlook common to all youth. It has meant well, even when it has misconceived its purpose. If it has provided a field in which numbers of men, blind to the Order's real significance, have sought merely social amusement and personal distinction, it has also proved a source of light and guidance to many obscure souls not subject to those vanities and who have realized and profited by its implications, and some of who from the portal of the Craft, have passed on in silence to more advanced methods or colleges of spiritual instruction. A sacramental system is not invalidated by the default of those accepting its jurisdiction; and as saints often flourished in the Church amid most unsaintly conditions, so not a few Masons have won to the Light despite the surrounding darkness of their brethren.

But now is coming a change, and it is significant that it comes not from the higher ranks of the Craft where, with all desire for the Craft's best interests, every tendency is towards conservatism and the sufficiency of old standards, but from the rank. and file, from the younger, newer blood now flowing into the veins of the Order. It is, of course, not a movement even remotely resembling disaffection, but now, as never before, brethren in numbers are asking from Masonry bread of life; they are caring less and less for ceremonies and ancient usages unless these can be shown to have supporting justification; they look to the leaders and teachers of the Craft for, not a perpetual reiteration of complimentary but unsatisfying speeches, but for instruction in real Masonic light and wisdom.

The future of the Order cannot be appraised without reference to the general social life surrounding it; for it is not something apart and detached from that life but an integral element of it, and between the two there is perpetual interaction and reaction. The gradual disintegration of the churches affects the Craft, tending both to increase it numerically and to advance the exploration of its concealed spiritual resources. Religion will not die—the religious instinct can never die—nor will "the Church" in some form cease to exist and to fulfill a certain ministry. But today a supplementary form of ministry is required and Masonry can provide it. A regrouping and redistribution of energy is taking place, in the course of which we may come to find that that powerful psychological phenomenon, a new group-consciousness—the Masonic consciousness—has been in process of formation; a consciousness which may become in time as potent a factor as was the religious consciousness of medieval days, or as was the moral power of the Delphic mysteries during the seventeen centuries of their great influence.

When the time ripens, the mysteries—as a science of life and an art of so living as to qualify for attaining ultra-natural life—will come to be restored. For long past, both within and without the church, the tide of human persuasion and events has been deadest against the tradition of regeneration into that ultra-natural life, as originally taught and practiced. But that which has been, is that which, in the course of cyclic recurrence, shall be again, and upon a higher level of development than before. It is not that the Christian church is not a steward of the mysteries—or at least that portion of it which does not reject the authentic sacramental *signa* and channels through which those mysteries may be realized; but, from reasons too complex and lengthy here to detail, there has been failure on the human side to realize them as they are now presented, with the result that the Christian ecclesia has degenerated into a state analogous to that into which the pre-Christian mystery systems had fallen when the new era began. To the clear-seeing eye the narrative in the gospels, apart from all questions of historicity, is a drama of initiation written for that time, for every eye to see, and for every mind to profit by; for what previously had been but adumbrated and approached by a few individuals in the concealment of the mystery schools, became, at the incarnation, objectified, universalized and made generally accessible—in other words the gospels became a manual of initiatic instruction to the whole world according to the measure of individual capacity to receive it, notwithstanding that large tracts of knowledge remained unproclaimed in those gospels but were reserved for more private communication. The recurrent cycle of the church's year, with its feasts and fasts, its symbolic seasons pointing to inhibitions and expansions of the soul's consciousness, is a true chart of the path to be followed by those who themselves seek initiation under the mastership of the Great Hierophant and Exemplar of regenerative science; while in the sacrament of the altar is portrayed, albeit under different symbolism, the actual process of initiation and the same transmutative changes in the body and mind of the recipient as are emblematized to the Masonic candidate in the Craft degrees.

Truth remains static, although temporal expressions and ministries of it follow the temporal order, and are born and die. When this form of the mysteries becomes neglected or abused, or that steward of them decrepit or ineffective, another—in the divine providence and patience—stands ready to carry forward their torch; truth becomes

> . . . fulfilled in many ways
> lest one good custom should corrupt the world. [*]

The Masonic system was devised three centuries ago, at a time of general unrest and change, as a preparatory infant-school in which once again the alphabet of a world-old gnosis might be learned and an elementary acquaintance made with the science of human regeneration. However misunderstood and misapplied, however materialistically conceived, have been its rites, the soul and consciousness of every voluntary participant in them stands imperishably impressed with the memory of them. The maxim "Once a Mason, always a Mason" expresses an occult truth not realized by those who are unaware of the subjective value and persistence of one's deliberated objective actions; though the Church implies the same truth when it deems the act of sacramental baptism to bring a given soul within the fold of Christ for ever. In each case, and

---

[*]   Alfred, Lord Tennyson, "Morte d'Arthur" (1845), lines 241–242.

especially so when the deliberate will of the neophyte assents to the act, a new addition is made to the group-soul of the community into which the individual becomes incorporated; and, in the case of the Masonic initiate, the aggregate and volume of what we have termed the Masonic consciousness is enlarged. Reactions and consequences follow of a nature perhaps too abstruse to dilate upon here, but to which the Roman initiated poet referred in the well-known words:

> *Magnus ab integro saeclorum nascitur ordo.*
> *Iam redit et Virgo; redeunt Saturnia regna;*
> *Iam nova progenies coelo demittitur alto.*

> A majestic New Order of generations is born,
> Now Virgo returns, Saturn's reign reinstates—
> And now is a lineage from high heaven issued new! [†]

Meanwhile, tinctured and affected by this metaphysical influence from the subjective world, the work of the Craft proceeds within this bourne of time and place; beginning, as we have shown, crudely and following the grosser tendencies of the natural order, until a moment is reached when a new birth becomes possible. Then the natural gives way to the spiritual, and the great material organization, a "body prepared," becomes the requisite physical vehicle for a correspondingly great office as a minister of real wisdom.

Operative masonry preceded and became spiritualized into speculative, and the gross beginnings of the latter are now becoming sublimated into a more subtle conception and tending to a scientific mysticism at once theoretic and practical. We may look forward to the gradual increasing spiritualization of the Craft and to its becoming—in a future the nearness or dis-

---

[†] Virgil, *Eclogues*, 4, lines 5–7 (English translation by Shawn Eyer). This passage was the inspiration for the American motto, *Novus Ordo Seclorum*, "a new order of generations."—Ed.

tance of which no one can presume to indicate—the portal to a still more advanced expression of the sacred mysteries. For, foretold the Great Master, the time will surely come when in the present ways of neither this "mountain"—neither this church nor that Craft—nor any Jerusalem that now serves as a place of peace, will men worship the Universal Father, but after another manner and mystically, that is, after the manner of the eternal mysteries.*

The churches, therefore, may be left to continue to discharge their proper ministry, while those who feel the need of a larger science, an alternative and perhaps richer fare than the churches provide, may find it in the ancient gnosis to which Freemasonry serves as a portal of entrance. By following the path to which that portal leads, they may be brought to a deeper knowledge of themselves and of the mysteries of their own being; to which end, and which end alone, the Masonic Craft was designed.

That Craft will only become what its individual members make it. If they see in it only a ceremonial procedure, at such it will remain, and their initiation will be but one in name and not in fact. But if they strive to realize and make their own the living spirit and intention behind the outward rites and formal usages, the dramatized quest of Light and of the Lost Word may result for them in a blessed finding of that which they profess to seek, and what they find themselves they will become able to communicate to other seekers, until the Craft is justified of all its children, and itself becomes—as it was intended to become—a great light in a dark world.

---

* Wilmshurst is alluding to a mystical interpretation of a passage of the fourth gospel: "The time is coming when you will worship the Father neither on this mountain nor in Jerusalem. . . But the time is coming, indeed it is already here, when true worshipers will worship the Father in spirit and in truth." (John 4:21, 23)—Ed.

Postscript

AND now let me close this book, as every lodge is closed, in peace and concord with all my brethren, and with the ancient prayer that the Order may be preserved of God, and its members be cemented with every virtue.[*] If, in what has here been written, Masonry has been given a conception spiritualized beyond the measure of its common understanding, I have but followed the example of our ancient brethren, who, lifting up their eyes to hills whence cometh strength, wrought their Masonic work upon the highest eminences of the mind and discerned the mysteries of the Craft, not with eyes of the flesh, but with the vision and understanding of the spirit. And they it was who perpetuated for us of later time an Order and a Doctrine by the right interpretation and use of which we, too, might ascend where they had risen, and from the same Mount of Vision behold the same things that they had seen.

Few, perhaps, ascend to those high hills today, in this more than usually troubled and dark age. But some are ready and eager to do so, and for them especially it is that this book is written. All must ascend thither at last. But, at the moment, the world-spirit is dominant in all our institutions. Wisdom is little apparent; for want of vision the people perish; and the quest of Light has to be pursued under conditions of peculiar adversity. But there is a mystery of Darkness no

---

[*] In the Emulation Rite used by the United Grand Lodge of England, the Master prepares to close the lodge by saying "Before we close this Lodge, let us with all reverence and humility express our gratitude to the Great Architect of the universe, for favors already received, and may He *continue to preserve our Order* by cementing and adorning it with every moral and social virtue." (*The Complete Workings of Craft Freemasonry*, p. 22, emphasis added) While similar wording exists in most American rituals, the prayer for the divine preservation of the Craft is not typically explicit.—Ed.

less than one of Light, and, in the molding hands of the Great Architect of the House of Life, the darkness and the light are both alike and serve as twin pillars that, finally, will establish that House in strength.

Those, then, who cannot, or are not yet prepared to, mount the higher path of understanding the things of the Craft, must nevertheless be thought of in charity, and spoken of in faith and in hope. For, placed as we all are in different and unequal degrees of perception upon the checker-work floor of life, around all alike—black and white, wise and foolish, learned and uninformed—runs the unifying, surrounding skirt-work and border of a common Providence; about us all are flung the Everlasting Arms; while, from the mutual interplay of the light and darkness in us all, becomes gradually generated the realization of that Wisdom in which, even now, we are all one, though of that unity few as yet are conscious. And since Wisdom will at last be justified of all her children, we need not complain of her processes, which, as they work out through the ages to a beneficent conclusion, temporarily involve the sharp and painful contrasts that we find.

Twenty-four centuries ago, at a time of similar darkness and degeneracy to the present, an aged seer and golden-tongued poet, who through a long life had contemplated the ancient mysteries of Light and Wisdom, spoke of the difficulty of conveying them to a world not yet able to appreciate them; and yet recognized the truth that, in the opposition of the world-spirit to them, the divine purpose was nevertheless being effected. In sending forth this book, then, and exhibiting the mysteries of Masonry in a light towards which, doubtless, some who read it will not at once be responsive, let me appropriate that poet's words, and welcome any inappreciation of what I have written with the same serenity as his; the same confidence of forward-looking faith in its ultimate acceptance:

Knowledge, we are not foes!
  I seek thee diligently;
But the world with a great wind blows,
  Shining, and not from thee;
Yet blowing to beautiful things,
  On, amid dark and light;
Till Life, through the trammellings
  Of Laws that are not the Right,
Breaks, clean and pure, and sings
  Glorying to God in the height!

—Euripides, *Bacchae*[*]

---

*   Gilbert Murray (translator), *The Bacchae of Euripides* (London: George Allen, 1904), p. 61.

About the Author

Walter Leslie Wilmshurst (British, 1867–1939) is the author of many books and articles on the esoteric or philosophical aspects of Freemasonry. He became a Mason at age 22 and was an active Mason all his life, writing and lecturing widely on spiritual and Masonic topics. He was also a gifted poet, and three of his masterful lyrics appear in the *Oxford Book of English Mystical Verse*.

His most popular book, *The Meaning of Masonry*, was first published in 1922. It is an advanced work of Masonic philosophy which interprets the Craft from the perspective of a modern mystic. It was received with tremendous enthusiasm on both sides of the Atlantic, and Wilmshurst soon produced a sequel, *The Masonic Initiation*, one of the most beautiful writings ever published on the subject.

The Lodge of Living Stones, a special Masonic fellowship inspired by the powerful vision of the Craft expressed in this book, was founded in 1927 in Leeds under the author's direct mentorship and direction.

The journal of the Quatuor Coronati research lodge calls his work "a constant source of instruction and assistance to those who are seeking for that which was lost."

Today, W. L. Wilmshurst remains one of the most influential and engaging interpreters of the Masonic tradition.

AGAPA
MASONIC CLASSICS

Agapa Masonic Classics presents modern editions of important works relating to the history, philosophy, symbolism and interpretation of Freemasonry.

The Agapa logo is derived from the Mason's mark of SIR ROBERT MORAY (1608–1673), a Scottish soldier, scientist and founding member of the Royal Society. In 1641 he was initiated into Freemasonry and designated a pentagram with the Greek word *agapā*—"love"—around it as his personal mark. Sir Moray explained that the individual letters of ΑΓΑΠΑ in turn represent the five Greek words *anechô, gnôthi, agapā, pisteuei and apechô*—the verbs "to tolerate, to know, to love, to have faith" and "to receive in full." Thus, *agapā* neatly summarizes Freemasonry's profound aims and most cherished ideals.

For a complete catalog of titles available from Agapa Masonic Classics, visit the website of Plumbstone Books.

www.plumbstone.com

CPSIA information can be obtained
at www.ICGtesting.com
Printed in the USA
FFOW04n1204180117
31448FF